A Tramp on the Line

Harri's on Tour

by Carl H. Harrison

Copyright © 2013 by Carl H. Harrison
First Edition – May 2013

ISBN
978-1-4602-1934-8 (Hardcover)
978-1-4602-1935-5 (Paperback)
978-1-4602-1936-2 (eBook)

All rights reserved.

No part of this publication may be reproduced in any form, or by any means, electronic or mechanical, including photocopying, recording, or any information browsing, storage, or retrieval system, without permission in writing from the publisher.

Produced by:

FriesenPress
Suite 300 – 852 Fort Street
Victoria, BC, Canada V8W 1H8

www.friesenpress.com

Distributed to the trade by The Ingram Book Company

There are two things in life to remember. True happiness is only achieved when what you give exceeds what you receive and you can never fix anything with a ten pound hammer.

To my friend and guitar coach Terry Smith, who has resolutely held onto a dream and worked towards it unswervingly all his life, no matter what.

TABLE OF CONTENTS

1 . . . . Prologue and Preparation

8 . . . . Toronto to Buffalo

17 . . . . Buffalo to Kansas City

49 . . . . Kansas City to Albuquerque

88 . . . . Albuquerque to San Diego

128 . . . . San Diego to Portland

151 . . . . Corvallis

177 . . . . Home

180 . . . . Epilogue

ROUTE MAP

Trains ridden and stations travelled through (bold indicates where we boarded and disembarked):

1. **The Maple Leaf**:
Toronto-Union Station (Ontario), Oakville, Aldershot, St. Catharines, Niagara Falls-Grimsby, Niagara Falls (New York), Buffalo-Exchange Street and **Buffalo-Depew**

2. **The Lakeshore Limited**:
Buffalo-Depew, Erie (Pennsylvania), Cleveland (Ohio), Elyria, Sandusky, Toledo, Bryan, Waterloo (Indiana), Elkhart, South Bend, and **Chicago-Union Station** (Illinois)

3. **The Southwest Chief**:
Chicago-Union Station, Naperville, Mendota, Princeton, Galesburg, Fort Madison (Iowa), La Plata (Missouri), **Kansas City-Union Station**, Lawrence (Kansas), Topeka, Newton, Hutchinson, Dodge City, Garden City, Lamar (Colorado), La Junta, Trinidad, Raton (New Mexico), Las Vegas, Lamy, **Albuquerque**, Gallup, Winslow (Arizona), Flagstaff, Williams Junction, Kingman, Needles (California), Barstow, Victorville, San Bernadino, Riverside, **Fullerton**

4. **The Pacific Surfliner**:
Fullerton, Anaheim, Orange, Santa Ana, Irvine, Laguna Mission-Mission Viejo, San Juan Capistrano, San Clemente-Pier, Oceanside, Solana Beach, San Diego-Old Town, **San Diego**

5. **The Coast Starlight**:
Los Angeles-Union Station, Van Nuys, Simi Valley, Oxnard, Santa Barbara, San Luis Obispo, Paso Robles, Salinas, San Jose, Oakland-Jack London Square, Emeryville, Richmond, Martinez, Davis, Sacramento, Chico, Redding, Dunsmuir, Klamath Falls (Oregon), Chemult, Eugene, Albany, Salem, **Portland-Union Station**

Prologue and Preparation

Tramp (tramp) n. a vagrant; one who wanders from place to place aimlessly.

Reflection (re flek shun) n. 1. That which is reflected, as, one's reflection in a mirror: the coming back of rays, as reflection of light from a polished surface. 2. Reproach, blame, discredit, as, a reflection on his honesty. 3. Thought, esp. of a meditative backward-turning nature.

Webster's Unabridged Encyclopedic Dictionary, copyright 1957

What goes around comes around. In 2009 I convinced my friend Gary that a 100 mile walk in England alongside Hadrian's Wall seemed like a good idea. Three years later he called with his own.

It was spring 2011 when he offered up that a railway trip across the United States would be a great way to spend some time. Since I had talked him into walking across England I could hardly let long held preconceived notions about unfriendly Americans get in the way, especially as he volunteered to make all the arrangements. We agreed November would be suitable since our respective summer places would be closed up and Christmas preparations would be off in the future. We also assumed there would be no concerns offered up by our spouses. In fact they seemed only too happy to be shed of us for three weeks.

We are both sons of railway men and having each travelled by rail a few times we pompously thought we knew what we were in for. Since we would be spending a number of nights on the train we agreed with little discussion nor hesitation that there was no way we were going to suffer in coach. We would book a roomette or what I will refer to throughout by the posher term of compartment.

In late spring I contacted an old friend from my teens who had moved to Corvallis, Oregon in the 1980's. Corvallis is an hour and a half from Portland where we had tentative plans to end the journey. Neil graciously offered a place to stay for a few days, which allowed the added bonus of he and I catching up with lives lived. While we had remained in contact over the years by email and Christmas cards I had only seen him three or four times in 30 years. Our timetable was such that Neil invited us to spend the American Thanksgiving holiday with him, his wife Azizah and their two kids. He really didn't have much choice as we were going to be there for the holiday anyway. He couldn't very well make us leave the house during dinner. Being nothing if not frugal, Gary and I leapt at the chance of free accommodations. In our previous three decades as bankers frugality had been daily pounded into us until we well understood how not to spend our own money. This history, added to our now being starving pensioners meant any offer of free accommodation - and food to boot - was not to be overlooked nor dismissed lightly.

Since retiring Gary spends some of his time volunteering on a hospital board in Thunder Bay, Ontario and it happened he would be in Toronto on a conference at the beginning of November. We agreed to start the adventure November 8 with a day or two in Toronto. We would then depart from the famous Union Station just down a few blocks from the fancy Intercontinental Hotel on Front Street. Gary already had a room reserved there for his conference and we could enjoy the special rate offered up to those attending and staying on for a day or two afterwards.

So the nucleus of our plan was set. We would board the train in Toronto and disembark in Portland. Now all we had to do was fill in the little bit between. Happily the trip would come together with remarkable ease helped along by the occasional piece of luck dropping right in our way.

In late August we had our first lucky break. Gary and his lovely partner Kim are gregarious folk who are constantly meeting new friends. They were holidaying at Mackinaw Island in Michigan and as fate would have it they met a couple who lived in Kansas City, Missouri. Over a bottle or two of wine Gary outlined our upcoming travel plans to their new friends.

Amtrak was offering a special fare that allowed unlimited train travel in the United States over 30 days that let you get on and off the train three times. You only had to advise where, when and the length the stops were to be. At this time we were still kicking around a number of stop off destinations but had tentatively decided that Chicago seemed a good choice, as did Albuquerque and somewhere in California. Gary and Kim's new friends recommended their town and said they knew of a good steak house right next to the train station. In fact it turned out to be in the same building. We both like to eat and Kansas City had a good reputation for beef. That was all it took to bump Chicago off the list.

By September all plans were finalized. We would meet in Toronto, spend a day and a night then leave Union Station on November 10. We had decided rather arbitrarily on two nights in Kansas City, four in Albuquerque, three in San Diego, four in Corvallis with Neil and his family and then fly home from Portland, Oregon via Vancouver. Our only struggle - if you could even call it that - was the California stop. Gary had suggested a stop somewhere near San Francisco but acquiesced when I offered that San Diego was likely going to be a warmer destination. Since we were both too cheap to pay roaming charges for cell phone access Gary would bring along his Playbook to help us stay in daily contact with home, but we would bring our cell phones in case of emergency.

My daughter Sara gave me a red leather clad journal for the trip. She and my youngest, Erin, had given me a similar one to record my thoughts on the English trip. That month-long sojourn with Gary in 2009 was a walk alongside the 2,000 year old Roman built Hadrian's Wall that separated England from the Scots. The trip also included a visit to London and then a visit on my own to my birthplace of Hull, Yorkshire. That daily journal became *Harri's on Tour - A Tramp in England*, available online at www.harrisontour.com and at a number of book stores in and around my Winnipeg, Manitoba home. As a starving author I must take every opportunity to plug the work.

As our November departure date approached I spent hours packing and unpacking various bags to come up with the optimum combination. Over the course of a number of conversations Gary and I decided to travel as light as possible and forego traditional suitcases. We decided an easy to carry bag of some sort and a small knapsack would be best. I ultimately chose a red carry-all like a small duffel bag with handles. My employer had given it to me years ago as part of some promotional campaign and being festooned with CIBC logos it was easy to spot amongst more conservative traveler's baggage. I constantly used this bag during the summers when travelling back and forth to my cottage and found it to be very easy to pack a large amount while still being easy to carry. I also decided on my trusty black canvas World Famous backpack. It has been everywhere with me over the last 25 years, with the exception of the walk in England.

On that trip Sara, who has some small knowledge of backpacks and such suggested a more proper pack would be beneficial. She arranged for a nice sized frame-equipped bag that proved both useful and comfortable while walking. Since we were not planning on much hiking this trip I had reckoned my old canvas friend would suffice. I also struggled with what jacket to take. November meant winter was coming to Winnipeg and while Toronto weather is generally nicer than home it could still be a bugger. Considering that we were going to spend a lot of time on the train, that we would only risk coolish weather in Kansas City and with the potential for wet weather on the northwest coast I eventually opted for the same jacket that accompanied me along Hadrian's Wall. This was a green water repellant one with fleece lining.

In the course of my preparations I had picked up a baseball hat from the Hudson's Bay store for Neil. It had Canada boldly embossed on it and I hoped it would make him smile and fondly remember home. The trick would be to carry it my baggage for nearly two and a half weeks without crushing the life out of it.

My single-minded attention to detail was on clear view during these preliminaries. My lovely Lynn, as usual, had our home under renovation and our belongings were packed in boxes hither and yon around the house. I would spend hours looking for $4 in U.S. bills and a handful of American coins I knew I had left over from a trip to Mexico. I would not relent in my search and it made no difference that the Canadian and U.S. dollar were near par. I had to find the cash, and I did; all $5.43 of it.

November 8, 2011, Tuesday - heading for Toronto

I was up at 6:30am and in spite of packing the previous day I repacked everything. An hour and a half later Lynn and I were on our way to the new Winnipeg airport terminal whose grand opening had just occurred a few days earlier. We spent the drive to the airport talking about a European holiday planned for the coming April. That plan entailed my going to England on my own for a couple of weeks then meeting Lynn in Paris for a further two weeks. She has yet to retire from gainful employment so still has limits on the length of her holidays. We had spent the better part of the previous Monday morning on the phone with Aeroplan booking our flights. We both spend so much by credit card that we had accumulated sufficient points to fly business class to Europe, which is a very nice way to travel. But as everyone knows the process for actually redeeming points is neither pleasant nor easy.

Previous trips have taught that there is such a thing as too much planning. Over planning usually results in changes being made due to a host of unforeseen situations and circumstances. We did not want to fall into that trap again so our thoughts were to do a minimum of pre-booking in the early stages. The balance of our plans could then be fleshed out in a more rational, comfortable and stress-free manner over the fullness of time. So we had just booked the flights to Europe and home again. I find Heathrow Airport in London to be very cumbersome so booked my flight to England via Manchester and Charles de Gaulle Airport for Lynn's flight to Paris. Our return flights home were booked from Manchester. Just by early booking our main arrival and departure we discovered we had much more flexibility with our plans for the balance of the trip. It may have not been the most economical method but it certainly reduced stress levels. It was while booking the flights to and from Europe that we discovered the benefit packages offered up with our new credit cards were not all that they were made out to be. We considered that we might well have to switch back to previously held cards.

The new Winnipeg airport building is huge compared to the 1960s-era one it replaced. It reminded me of Calgary's airport and a couple of others with not too bold a design. Considering security needs I guess there are plenty of limitations when it comes to usefulness. By 9:00am we had said our goodbyes and I was on my way thorough security and my first bit of bother. I was required to take of my shoes, notwithstanding they were rubber soled and had never proved troublesome on a dozen previous trips. Then I was lucky enough to be chosen for a pat down (training purposes don't you know). When I finally got through security I had forgotten that I had put my wallet and belt into my backpack before going through in a misguided attempt to make things easier for myself. Once on the other side and while sorting myself out I discovered my wallet wasn't in my pants and I panicked for a second, although it seemed like 10 minutes at the time. The incident reminded me of Gary losing his wallet and passport on the English trip at a place called Saughy Rigg Farm. I may have been partially to blame for that incident and don't wish to go into details, but it turned out well in the end.

Then the first of many good omens popped up. My favourite fast food joint, Salisbury House, had a kiosk on the departure side of security where I bought a coffee and two of their famous chocolate-covered donuts. I also offered my place in line to a flight attendant who was clearly in a rush and needed some breakfast. No good deed goes unrewarded, plus she was kind of cute. While waiting I noticed that prices were slightly elevated for the captive market from what was charged at their other places around town. It made no difference to me as the brief repast was just what I needed.

Toronto to Buffalo

It was an easy two hour flight to Toronto and I spent time reading and even more time thinking about a cheap way to the Intercontinental Hotel. We arrived on time at 1:45pm and 30 minutes later and $23.95 poorer I was on the Airport Express Shuttle with the Intercontinental being the third stop. And then some luck, as my checking in coincided with Gary's day of meetings ending.

There was a spectacular view from the 20th floor room. The rail yards were nearly adjacent to the hotel and we were overlooking Lake Ontario and Toronto Island. I could see planes coming and going from the small airport out on the island. Gary regularly travels from Thunder Bay to Toronto on Porter Airlines, which flies out of that airport. Porter also runs a free airport shuttle from the island airport to downtown which takes a fraction of the time it takes to get from Pearson International. I should have been so lucky.

We caught up a bit as I unpacked and sorted myself out before heading out for a drink. But before the drink we walked the three short blocks to Union Station to get the lay of the land and confirm departure requirements. We are nothing if not organized and are both particularly careful about ensuring we know exactly what is what when travelling.

Union Station was an enormous edifice as would be expected for Canada's largest city, with trains and commuter subways arriving and departing continually throughout the day and throngs of people milling about in mid afternoon. We would come to pass through four train stations on our journey that identified themselves as Union Stations. All were built at the beginning of the 1900s in the same grand style and shared the same name because they accommodated all the various railway companies tooling about North America at the time.

Our keen sense of direction and an enormous sign ensured we readily found our departure gate. After asking a number of people as well as double checking with the ticket agent we ensured that arrival at the gate half an hour prior to departure would be quite sufficient. We are both fairly consistent in our travelling habits and prefer getting to departure gates when requested by the professionals in charge, since spending down time in the lounge beats the alternative of running madly for gates. But train travel was different and we were to learn that it was much more laid back. While this and every subsequent stationmaster wanted you there 30 minutes before departure my sense was that you could arrive as the train was leaving the platform and not be too much of a bother to anyone. This likely had something to do with the dynamics of living and breathing train schedules. While trains occasionally seemed to leave on time there were a couple of instances where our train was late leaving a station and a number of instances when delays appeared while we were aboard. Happily, delays caused by breakdowns or passing freight trains never bothered us on board as we were blissfully unhampered by any real need to be anywhere. That said, sitting in train stations on uncomfortable chairs in 100 year old stations occasionally alongside odd people could get old fast. We discovered that strange people tend not to fly - they take the train. While everyone has the right to travel as they wish, sitting beside someone who's having a conversation with a chair can cause one discomfort.

We had by now slipped quickly into our usual practice when together of a glass of beer or wine each afternoon to aid digestion. After leaving the station we stopped for a drink at sports bar we had both been to separately before, much like "going to separate schools together." The Loose Moose was conveniently located just out the door and down from our hotel. The waitresses wore white leggings, which along with their short skirts seemed to catch and hold our attention. While not a follower as such I have always considered myself a student of fashion trends so my careful review of the waitresses should be rightly considered as nothing more than research. This bar was where Gary set the tone for the trip. He would generally have wine and I would have beer or a gin and tonic.

Later that evening we walked to an Elephant & Castle Restaurant a few blocks away for dinner and a few (more) drinks. It was a good meal and a great start to some unexpectedly terrific meals we would enjoy throughout the trip. Afterwards we wandered back to the hotel and decided a drink in the bar was in order. We each had one with Gary also having an espresso, which apparently helps him sleep. The bill came to an astronomical $30 with my shot of gin being $12. This was not a great way to start an economical holiday. In fairness, the Intercontinental was a fairly upscale hotel and well beyond either of our usual styles. We had both travelled extensively on our own and at our previous employer's expense so we should not have been surprised at what things cost. That said we resolved not to fall victim to such larceny again.

Later that night we watched Howard Hawks' final western of his John Wayne trilogy, *Rio Lobo*, on television. It was remarkably clear why it was the last one.

November 9, Wednesday

The morning plan was to meander down to a Starbucks we had already scoped out for a hot drink and a light breakfast at 7:00am. I would then read the paper until Gary's conference finished sometime in the late morning. We both needed to find an ATM and there was also a need to find a bottle of medicinal brandy for the train.

Gary's conference ended earlier than anticipated and we were out the door and on our way into the heart of Toronto by 11:00am. First thing up was a walk by the lakefront and the promenade alongside. Incredibly, in dozens of visits to Toronto Gary had never been to the lakefront, whereas I make a practice of going there every time I am in the city. He does awake each morning to views of the ocean that is Lake Superior whereas I awake to oceans of wheat so I could understand his indifference to Lake Ontario. We tramped about for an hour or so and as it was approaching a traditional meal time Gary had a plan and we ended up at Fran's on Front Street. Fully refreshed we walked up Yonge Street for a number of blocks and then crossed over to University Avenue just before the Ontario Legislature buildings. The temperature was a pleasant 12C and very nice for walking. The half pint with lunch was pleasant but was by now pressing so we stopped in at a Second Cup coffee shop to dispense and refill. We had by now acquired a bottle of French brandy that turned out to be the best of the number we bought and disposed of over during the trip.

We continued to walk about in a somewhat meandering route back towards the hotel.

OUT THE HOTEL WINDOW TO LAKE ONTARIO WITH TORONTO ISLAND IN THE DISTANCE

Upon our return we spent part of the late afternoon in the hotel room reading the papers and checking emails. Much to my delight I discovered an email from McNally Robinson Booksellers who had recently agreed to place *A Tramp in England* on their shelves. They were requesting some information and computer-related details from me to help market the book. While I am not quite a Luddite when it comes to technology I do know my limitations and they were reached with this request. I emailed my book and web designer, Steven Downie and passed the note on to him while asking for his gracious assistance, and he didn't disappoint. It was all very exciting.

Once this and other correspondence was dealt with we went out for another coffee at Starbucks. Rain was soon pelting down so our exploration of downtown Toronto was done. It was still raining later that evening when we walked back across to the convenient

Loose Moose for dinner. Afterwards it was still chucking it down so hard that all we could do was go back to the hotel. We prudently decided we couldn't afford $12 shots so opted to pack up our bags for the morrow while having a brandy and watching television.

Our plan was to get up at 6:00am and have coffee in the room. We had wisely bought a couple of cakes and muffins at Starbucks for the morning. We would then head for Union Station so as to be onboard 20 minutes before the 8:20am departure.

It's all in the planning.

I slept okay but as on the previous night I found myself momentarily awake at 3:00am. I thought it likely the rail yards and associated noise 20 stories below the window woke me.

November 10, Thursday – heading for Buffalo aboard The Maple Leaf

We were up and at 'em by 6:00am and after coffee and check out were out the door by 7:15. Ten minutes later we were in Union Station standing by gate 16 near the middle of the waiting area for our train; actually it was the middle of the station's main tunnel passageway. It is lucky that we both have the same thoughts when it comes to arriving for transportation departures - better half an hour early than five minutes late. There were fewer than a dozen travelers in front of us and we were next to last in line, but in less than 20 minutes there were nearly 50 people behind us. Various trains were disgorging passengers into the tunnel and we soon found ourselves standing rock still in a stream of people going past in both directions, like a scene from a 1960s Italian movie. The lady behind us was on her way to St. Catharines and she gave us the lowdown on the rules of the rails. She chatted incessantly and with the odd probing question from Gary we soon discovered that she was originally from St. Catharines but worked in Toronto. She had recently purchased a house in her home town where she intended to retire and was on her way down there to close the deal. Apparently buying a home in Toronto was unthinkable.

At exactly 8:00am there was an announcement over loudspeakers that those needing assistance boarding should please step forward and proceed through the doorway and up to the tracks. The first couple in line was a pushy woman and her dapper husband who took this to mean they could proceed. She didn't need assistance so must have assumed that the rules didn't apply to her. Clearly she was not a Canadian as we are much too polite. She was indignant when told to go back in line and wait until those who needed assistance were boarded. They returned to the line much to their chagrin and the amusement of the rest of us. We had not seen the last of this woman and she would get her comeuppance a few miles down the rails.

Just a few minutes later we were asked to board and were quickly and capably directed onto the right coach. Promptly at twenty five past eight we were underway and just as promptly Gary was off in search of a cup of coffee. The schedule said an hour and a half to the border with arrival in Buffalo at 1:30pm. Looking back it is amazing how naïve we were.

The train spent a good deal of time rolling alongside Lake Ontario and with the weather clear and bright sightseeing out the window was quite pleasant. We did have reserved seats but there were only about 20 passengers in the day coach so there was lots of room. Six months later I would be in England taking advantage of their rail system. While their train service is second to none I can unequivocally state that if you travel by day coach a reserved seat is much more calming on the nerves than running with the pack to search out the three unreserved seats in a carriage.

Our schedule suggested we would reach the border crossing just past Niagara Falls at 10:37am and we weren't disappointed. It also said the stop would be five minutes long - it wasn't. At **11:37** we were still stopped and my lifelong trepidation around crossing the U.S. border was on high alert. Of the 20 passengers aboard the four border guards had identified five they were not happy about and they were taken off the train for more intense "documentation reviews." Happily we were not in that elite group. One of the unlucky five was the pushy woman from the front of the line in Toronto; karma really is a bitch.

There was also a passenger who was strangely not asked to get off. She was an elderly Japanese woman and when the young border guard asked her if she had any fruits or vegetables to declare, she said no, no, no. There was a grocery bag on the seat beside her and the guard asked her again, and again she said no, no, no. He asked at least five times always getting a negative response in triplicate. In exasperation he said he had no choice but to check the bag, which suddenly seemed to trouble the lady and she said no, no, no. Upon opening the bag he exclaimed "you have avocados and walnuts" to which she shrugged. He pointed out that she should not have lied to him because now he had no alternative but to check her suitcase which upset her even more. You could see it coming, another dozen avocados in the suitcase. The clearly exasperated guard bagged up the fruit and nuts and took them with him as he walked away shaking his head. Five minutes later the lady was standing beside her seat hyperventilating. I asked her if she wanted some water as I thought a heart attack was imminent but she said no, no, no. She quickly recovered from the loss of the produce but I am unsure if she understood the seriousness of the situation she had put herself in. The potential for water boarding at Guantanamo Bay loomed large in my imagination.

She was luckier than the Niagara Five; they were escorted off the train. One was dressed like a rapper and had confessed loudly to a criminal record and was travelling with his dad. Another was an ex British navy sailor living off a girlfriend in Kansas City who claimed he had been in Toronto for a week's holiday. Then there was the aforementioned pushy woman and two others who seemed quite normal. All were permitted back on the train in due course so likely their problems were more related to documentation than anything overly serious. With all the well-known concerns around security in the U.S. you would think people would be fully prepared for a border check and that they would have all their ducks lined up.

During our lengthy wait (scheduled for five minutes but which stretched into two and a half hours) the conductor regularly passed through the carriage advising that we would be on our way shortly. He stopped to chat with most passengers and mentioned in the most serendipitous manner to ensure that we should get off at the second train stop in Buffalo. He stressed the second stop not the first. He also told us that he didn't envy our layover in Buffalo as there was absolutely nothing to do there and he recommended that we walk to a shopping mall 20 minutes from the station for diversion.

Finally just before 1:00pm we were shufflin' off to Buffalo just an hour away. Gary had bought a cheese plate when he bought his coffee first thing upon boarding in Toronto and now peckish again he finished it off; none had been offered then nor would be offered now to his travelling companion. Another half dozen passengers had joined us at the border crossing but the carriage was still half empty and it had turned grey and rainy outside. We reached Buffalo and disembarked as advised at the second stop in the suburb of Depew. I have no doubt that if left to our own devices we would have jumped off at the first station and then experienced all the sorrows that would have brought down upon us. Strangers in a strange land and all that.

BUFFALO TO KANSAS CITY

There was an unusual reason we had to travel right through Buffalo to catch our westbound connection. A number of ancient viaducts and bridges over the tracks in Buffalo were too low for the double-decker Amtrak rail cars to pass under. The problem must have been obvious when the new two level carriages were built nearly 50 years ago. The solution to this little problem was an additional station for westbound traffic constructed in Depew that turned out to be the size of a bungalow. It was clearly built as a second thought to quickly correct the issue around double-decker passenger cars but you'd think that sometime during the intervening years a more impressive building would have been erected.

This stop would prove to be our longest wait between trains. It was scheduled for eight hours and somehow that long wait time had not registered in our consciousness during the euphoria of planning the trip. The actual wait would stretch out even longer and it would soon seem like a lifetime. In hindsight, if we had disembarked at the first station in Buffalo we could have used the confusion that would no doubt have entailed to kill off some time in the making of arrangements to get to the Depew depot. It was what it was and being veteran travelers we were not going to be out done by a little thing like a long wait so we checked our bags, which included my glasses. I could say that I had wanted to keep them safe but that would not be entirely accurate. I only really need them to see so I of course thought I could manage without them. Happily Gary was around to decipher between phone booths and taxi cabs.

We confirmed with the train agent that the conductor's recommended mall was a good spot to spend some time and as it was raining softly we took a $14 cab ride there. You will remember that the conductor had told us the mall was close by. Just right out the station door he said, then left at the highway, a 20 minute walk at most he said, no problem. Well, while the directions were accurate it turned out to be a near 20 minute cab ride. If we had tried to walk it in the rain it could have well been a disaster. On the other hand it would have used up a lot of time so perhaps it might not have been such a bad plan.

The upscale centre was quite busy with shoppers when we arrived. Since it was time for something to eat and considering where we were we thought Buffalo wings. We chose a sports bar within the mall and I had a beer and Gary wine. Après wings and drinks we decided we could only spend so much time wandering about a mall so decided a movie would be a reasonable way to spend some of the remaining seven hours. We saw *Tower Heist* with Eddie Murphy; contrary to some reviews I read later it was not bad and I am not really a fan. After the film we went to a brew pub on the grounds of the shopping centre and as Gary had brought along his Playbook we took the opportunity of free wifi to successfully sign on to our respective emails. During the trip we could usually find somewhere at least a couple of times a day where we could sign on and stay in touch with home. It is amazing technology. One of my emails that night was from the bookstore to say that they had heard from my designer and they had just put my book's details on their website. We had a look and when Gary said that it looked cool it made my day.

When we just couldn't sit in the bar anymore we went back to the mall and came across a tobacconist's shop that had only been opened a couple of weeks. I am honestly unsure what with the prevailing climate regarding tobacco and smoking how a smoke shop can survive these days. Gary did help them out by buying a couple of cigars and some accessories. The clerk tried to sell him a $10 cigar cutter to which Gary had said no thanks whereupon the guy gave it to him. We both considered this to be an unusual sales technique.

We continued our mall walk and discovered a Cheesecake Factory where in spite of my having one more cup of coffee and Gary a glass of Ruffino we found we were beginning to slow down. We called for a cab and were back at the Depew station by 9:45pm and in good time for our train, plenty of time as it turned out. We retrieved our bags and sat in the plastic chairs in the small-ish waiting room that was fast filling up with travelers including a 14-year-old girls' hockey team, all their parents and assorted hangers on. I now had my glasses so could see what was going on around me.

I noticed a challenged young man in his early 20s who was clearly not waiting on a train. He was wearing a Locomotive Engineers Operators Union bomber jacket with obvious pride. It was clear that he liked being in the station and with the people working there. He must have been a regular visitor because even at that late hour the staff and attendants all took the time to laugh and chat with him. He and the man I assumed was a relative or at least a caregiver were there for four hours that night.

My Erin has her own challenges and I think I am aware of the determination that young man had to muster to get to the point where he was comfortable as a regular visitor and then to make friends as well. Without doubt the folks at the station made it easier for him. While sitting watching I recalled an episode in my daughter's life where her determination and other people's support were on display. She was about 13 and at a school sports day. She and a friend had entered a four-lap run around the oval field. The two took off with the pack and, as expected, before too long were bringing up the rear and quite off the pace. All was going well until the bulk of the pack crossed the finish line and Erin and her friend still had more than half a lap to go. You could see from the stands that they were both exhausted.

Her friend had clearly had enough so she decided to call it a day and crossed over the infield to the finish line. I could see my girl was distraught but she was doggedly continuing on, but she had started to cry. My heart was breaking as I walked across the infield and up beside her. Trying to provide some measure of support I told her she had done wonderfully and it was alright if she wanted to stop. Through tears and sobs she said no she was going to continue on to the finish line. Between my own tears I asked her if I could walk with and to my surprise she said yes. At the finish line waiting for us was a group of her classmates, helpers and teachers and all were cheering her on. We finished the race together five minutes after the pack and by the time we got to the line she was grinning and laughing. Not for the first time in my life I was beaming proud to be pointed out as the dad of that remarkable young woman.

The young man at the station was enjoying himself yet those of us awaiting on the train were not nearly as content. There were not enough chairs for everyone and aside from a couple of vending machines and washrooms there were no amenities. This was not what you would expect for folks taking the train to Chicago and points west. I was really beginning to flag, where was the train, it was already an hour late?

At 11:30pm it was announced that the Lakeshore train was going to be 52 minutes late. Actually it was already an hour late; this announcement made it two hours late. Schedule-wise Gary and I had no problems since we had a five hour layover in Chicago, but I confess to a momentary pause around Gary and his arrangement making. True to form and fully meeting expectations came the announcement 50 minutes later that the train had just left Rochester, 50 minutes away. No oops or sorry, just that we could now expect to depart at 1:00am. Gary was starting to get a little testy but strangely I had settled down. I had Zenned myself to inner peace while he opined that if the train was any later we wouldn't need a sleeper and a refund would be in order.

November 11, Friday – heading for Kansas City on The Lakeshore Limited

We finally boarded at 2:00am. Our first roomette of the trip was smaller than either of us had expected and our first impressions were not good. Strangely and happily 10 minutes later neither of us had any issues with the accommodations nor would have any going forward. I think we had both expected compartments to be like the ones in the James Bond movies - facing sets of side by side armchairs. We would discover that there are such things but they are called rooms and accommodate up to four travelers. They cost twice as much, which seemed fair as they were twice as big.

The compartment was likely a metre and a half wide and just over two metres long, large enough for the two comfortable facing armchairs with high seat backs, like a Queen Anne chair mated with La-Z-Boy. There was a fold-down table between the seats that we would seldom utilize, and about half a metre of space between the arms of the chairs and the wall separating us from the passageway. This wall had windows on both sides of a sliding glass door, all with thick curtains. I should note that on all the trains we rode the compartment doors would magically announce that they were not properly latched by sliding open, though not right away mind. The doors would give us the benefit of the doubt. Sometimes they would open minutes after we had thought we had shut them or sometimes they would wait half an hour or even longer before alerting us.

This first compartment had a small closet beside one of the chairs with room to hang up two facecloths or handkerchiefs dependent on needs. The opposite side had an ingenious set up that at first look appeared to be a couple of steps to allow access to the upper berth. On closer inspection it was discovered that the higher second step flipped down into a stainless steel wash basin with cold running water with the lower step flipping up to reveal a toilet. Ingenious engineering for a toilet perhaps but frankly not a facility of which I would ever have considered utilizing, even if I had been travelling on my own. Subsequent compartments down the line did not have the benefit of the toilet but did retain the wash basin. The compartments also had power outlets to charge laptops or razors and such and there were also reading lights similar to those found on airplanes and a couple of small lights in the ceiling. In the evenings the facing armchairs folded down with seats and backs cushions forming the lower berth. The upper berth was hidden in a portion of the ceiling that was hinged to the wall. It was simply pulled down when needed and was a single mattress which I would find more comfortable than the lower four-cushion mattress. You could not comfortably stand in the compartment when the upper berth was pulled down.

It would prove very cumbersome to get in and out of the upper and I was amazed at the numbers of people on the train who were heavier, older or both who clearly would struggle to get up there. Once in either bed though it was quite comfortable and there was plenty of room in each, as long as you didn't want to move or turn over. The upper also had a web-like contraption to prevent the occupant from falling out at night. Falling out would have been disastrous since if one did fall it would have been near impossible to hit the floor. You would have ended up at best as a crumpled ball lodged suspended above the floor jammed between the closet and toilet. I joke - the accommodations while tight were pleasant and comfortable.

The luxury to stretch out after a lifetime in Depew was something we had both been looking forward to and we toasted liberally with our first brandy of the night. Whilst enjoying the small tot we mutually agreed that while unexpected and given that it might possibly prove handy, there was no way either of was going to use the toilet. Later I took the upper berth and soon settled in and watched the moonlit nightscape out the window for half an hour. The train was remarkably quiet with none of the expected clickitty clack. There was an occasional side to side swaying of the carriage which was likely due to its height and the centre of gravity but I slept great. This would turn out to be our only train with window views from the upper berth, and so alternating or the flipping of a coin for the upper became necessary.

Scheduled arrival time in Chicago was 10:30am and we were awakened by our porter banging about at 7:00am. Actually there had been a time zone change so it was an hour earlier. Like all but one of our porters on the trip this guy was as big as a football linebacker. How he managed to move around and work in the cramped surroundings of the compartments was amazing to watch. We learned the hard way that he was an aspiring rap star.

Time zone changes on the train were quite the convoluted process. They were acknowledged and we were pre-warned about them but time zone changes did not impact the dining room schedule. In short you were best advised not to change your watch when you went to bed since breakfast reservations were always based on the previous day's time zone. This was occasionally confusing and I likely have not adequately explained it but I believe it had something to do with the crew timetable.

At our first onboard breakfast we were made aware of the universal train rule that everybody shares table space. Each table had four settings and people were placed at every spot if required and in our experience it was usually always required. To be fair they didn't split guests up and if you were in a party of three you would always be seated together. But if there were only two of you they would always sit at least one stranger at your table. On this first morning we ate with a gentleman from Pakistan who now lived in Chicago. He had boarded at Depew and decided to get a compartment at the last minute and likely paid twice what we had as a result of this last minute decision. That was about all I could comprehend from his thick accent but according to Gary's expert deciphering he apparently found the accommodations quite claustrophobic. Our dining companion was quite polite but I had a sense that he thought he was intruding by sitting with us, which he wasn't. Maybe it was just his pleasant old world politeness coming across.

The breakfast was well presented and prepared and the tea was drinkable, which was totally beyond my expectations. We weren't rushed out but there were people waiting so we went back to our compartment to watch the world go by. It was a totally grey day with snow-covered fields and a dreary view to say the least. An announcement stated we would arrive in Chicago an hour and a half late and since we had set off from Depew two hours late I was skeptical. Perhaps trains like airplanes do not go as fast as they can. Perhaps there is always something in reserve just in case a burst of speed is required to arrive nearly on time.

After the first day's delays at the border and Depew I made the decision to take announcements made around arrival and departure times as nothing more than suggestions. Wishful thinking perhaps and definitely not something one should necessarily rely on. I hoped such an attitude would ensure I wouldn't get wound up when schedules were not met. It did seem to work out that way.

During the excellent breakfast our compartment had been converted to armchairs and they were quite comfortable. The chairs faced each other and with plenty of foot room one could stretch out without bothering your travelling companion. There was a common washroom three doors down and on the car's lower level there were two more plus a couple of shower cubicles. We had jammed our bags into whatever nook and cranny we could and were settled in reasonable comfort. There were no thermostat controls in any of our compartments but we never had any complaint about the temperature. We didn't know it then but we could have placed our bags in a storage compartment on the lower level. When we became aware of the storage opportunity on a later train we still didn't take advantage. We both liked to keep our eyes on our stuff which now seems odd as I have absolutely no problem in checking everything whenever I fly.

We found we had little reason to complain about being crowded when in the compartment, that is to say when we were sitting down or settled in the berths. When not settled it seemed like you had to go outside to the passageway to exhale and especially if we both happened to be standing upright at the same time. We soon quite naturally adapted a process whereby the first one in the compartment quickly sat down giving the other the opportunity to enter.

The train was quite full and traffic in the carriage was constant. While the passageway was wide enough for one if you met someone coming the other way both had to turn sideways to pass. A couple of times over the course of the trip when meeting a well-girthed passenger I opted to step into an open compartment to avoid a close encounter of the third kind.

One of the first things we noted of the Windy City as we neared the downtown station was a number of people living under a highway underpass. One was wrapped up in a blue plastic tarpaulin trying to catch some sleep, another was getting out of a tent and the third was playing checkers against himself on an upturned cardboard box. The train was temporarily stopped at this point and I watched him make a few moves, from both sides of the board. Home is where it is.

They call the area we had just travelled through and would be travelling through for another day yet the Rust Belt. It really was quite something to see all the enormous buildings that were once factories and warehouses now standing idle and falling to dust. There seemed miles of derelict buildings as we passed through cities and towns from Buffalo to well past Chicago. The numbers of jobs they once housed and which have now gone away must be staggering. Whatever it was they had generated in these places was now manufactured elsewhere at a cheaper cost. Demand hadn't gone away, just the jobs. We all want to buy our stuff cheaper and never mind the social cost. This is progress I guess and there is a lesson there somewhere.

CHICAGO

We arrived in that toddlin' town on time at noon (depending on your perspective as to what 'on time' was) and were immediately on the lookout for a place to eat. The Chicago station is one of the largest in the U.S. and was packed with people coming and going, yet we were completely at ease wandering about the grand old building. It helped that our baggage was so easily managed. We found a nice buffet type of spot right in the station and while it was very busy we readily got our meals and easily found a place to sit. During our lunch conversation I felt Gary was micro-planning to ensure all eventualities were covered. It was totally unnecessary for him to stress as the plans he'd made were all perfect, the stuff in our control that is, and everything was going swimmingly. Gary would let go somewhat and start to be more relaxed over the following few days.

We were booked on a day coach for our next jaunt and by 1:10pm we were sitting in the waiting room awaiting the 3:00pm Southwest Chief which would drop us off in Kansas City on its travels to Los Angeles. We would get back on the Chief after the stop in Kansas City, then off at Albuquerque and on again one last time for the final run to Los Angeles. Interestingly the dining car menus would remain the same throughout our time on the Chief. There was nothing wrong with the meals it just seemed odd that the menu would remain the same over our four different trips on the same line.

While waiting we spent a little time talking about plans for Kansas City and Albuquerque. As usual we were both on the same page. Gary and I know each other well and have travelled together enough that we trust each other's judgment and that makes travelling life easier. Soon we formed some rudimentary plans and with still an hour before boarding I spent my time using the Playbook to send off emails while Gary went off in search of a cup of coffee and a bottle of water.

Once boarded and underway way the views out the window were again of decaying manufacturing infrastructure in the urban areas, but also of bucolic farm fields and some small treed areas when away from towns. We did notice a preponderance of old car wrecking yards like we used to have at home. Places I used to relish visiting and crawling through when I was a kid looking for used parts for my heap of the month. Now the wrecking yards at home are computerized and the wrecks have a limited shelf life and after a couple of months whatever is left is sent to the shredder as scrap. Here, from what we could see there appeared to be little in the way of disposal for old vehicles. In fact in a day or two we would be passing through numerous communities where it seemed civic bylaws required anyone with property alongside the rail line had to maintain at least two derelict vehicles.

By half past four we were out in the country. Flat, flatter, flattest land I'd ever seen, flatter even than Saskatchewan. We passed by wind farms with dozens of turbines standing at attention. With the sun going down the turbines' outlines on the horizon against the golden sunset was quite something. Strangely, none of them were turning. There were miles of uninterrupted fields and it appeared to this adopted prairie boy that the majority of crops were off but there were still a couple of areas where corn and wheat were still to be harvested.

I mentioned we were now travelling in a coach which of course meant we had to look after our own meals so we decided to buy dinner to 'pass the time.' Gary was not going to miss a meal no matter the cost so the dining car seemed like a better idea than the club car and microwaved hamburgers. I opted for baked chicken with creamed mashed potatoes. The chicken was good but someone should have been arrested for the potatoes. They were likely peeled, boiled and freeze-dried during the Clinton administration and probably his first term at that. I don't care for whipped potatoes at any time but these were like gruel and I suspected they came out of a box. The $20 touch seemed an outrage and I recall this as the only truly bad meal I had on the entire journey, either on or off the train. I am sure that the fact it was the only train meal I had to pay for was purely coincidental.

While dining we reached a milestone. At a quarter to seven we crossed the mighty Mississippi River and I suddenly recalled a jingle we'd been taught at school to help learn how to spell Mississippi. I hadn't thought of that little ditty in a very long time but as a learning tool it certainly worked and I sang it in my head as we crossed the river. We rolled on through the American heartland passing through small town after small town separated by miles of open land. The beautiful countryside outside my window was further enhanced by a sunset which started about 4:30pm and lasted a good hour and a half. A cleverer man than I would be able to adequately explain how travelling west at 100 km/hour stretched the sunset out as long as it did.

We arrived in Kansas City at 9:50pm, a full 20 minutes ahead of schedule and a pleasant surprise after our first couple of trains. We were tired and of course disorientated but we knew from our booking information that the hotel was within walking distance. Naturally we hadn't a clue in what direction to head so we asked a couple of security guards in the station the way to the hotel. We were looking for the Hyatt Regency Crown and the first guy we asked clearly did not speak Canadian as he had no clue what we were talking about. Happily the second knew where we wanted to get to and said we could get there by way of the overhead walkway that connected the station with office buildings, a number of hotels and shopping centres in the area. The walkway was meant to protect residents from inclement weather. Haughtily I suggest people in Kansas City have no idea what inclement weather is; for that you must travel to Winnipeg, Manitoba.

We wandered about up and down stairs, along corridors, through raised walkways attached to the outside of buildings and over the city streets for what seemed like ages. We asked directions a number of times from passersby and maintenance men until finally a fellow closing up a restaurant said "through those doors and up the stairs then just follow the walkway." We had already been doing just that for quite some time.

Once found, our destination turned out to be a lovely huge hotel with an enormous four-storey atrium serving as the front lobby. We learned later that 20 or so years past there had been a terrible accident. The atrium had been designed with walkways from one side to the other on floors two and three. At a festive gathering with people dining and dancing on the walkways they gave way and collapsed killing a number of people. You would have expected that such a tragedy would have meant the end of the hotel but it didn't. The walkways were rebuilt and now the collapse is just an interesting footnote in the history of the hotel.

We were checked in by a young clerk who looked to be 10 months pregnant and who I am afraid, and bless her heart, was not very bright. She asked an incredible amount of questions about where we were from and guided by the puzzled look on her face I'd swear she had no idea where Canada was in relation to her home country. It is even quite possible that she had never heard of Canada. She was not alone with geographic issues though, as I was unsure if Kansas City was in Kansas or in Missouri. I of course assumed the obvious and was wrong.

Our kind but confused reception clerk did manage to let us know that while wifi was free in the lobby there was a charge for it in the room. Being as always on limited and tightish budgets we opted for the free option and would soon discover why it was free. Access was spotty at best and getting reception sometimes involved standing on one foot with the other in the air. It was kind of like trying to get rabbit ear antennas to tune in television reception in the good old black and white days.

Since it had been a hectic couple of hours we determined it would be in order to have a drink in the hotel bar which was packed with 40 guys and two old women. The television was on and we overheard that 30-year fixed mortgages could be had for 3.25%. How the Americans have any problems with housing costs is beyond me. I mean 30 years with fixed rates of 3.25% and said interest tax deductible to boot! Two gins (me) and two red wines (Gary) later we were calmed and relaxed. I note that this was a fairly upscale place and certainly on par with the Intercontinental in Toronto. Our two drinks here cost less than the one each we'd had there.

There was also a bit of strangeness that evening. A passenger had got on the train with us in Chicago wearing a complete Chicago Cubs baseball uniform. We were to see him a couple of times over the next few days and each time he was in the same attire. It seemed odd to us but we thought it must have been some sort of promotion. But if a promotion would you expect he would wear it all the time? We had already seem some strange people in this country and it did cross our minds that maybe he just liked wearing the uniform. My mother's son did wonder if he only had the one suit, how did he keep it clean.

Once settled in the room Gary called the couple he and Kim had met on Mackinaw Island and arrangements were made for dinner the next evening. Gary sensed they seemed tentative on the phone and this would have been totally understandable. They had only met Gary and Kim the once and they had never met me and here we were in town looking to have dinner with them. A brandy later we talked about how relaxing it had been on the train and a professional might have taken that to mean we were not exactly relaxed in Kansas City. We kicked around what we were going to do the next day and I had to insist that there was no need to set the alarm to wake us on the morrow

November 12, Saturday

We awoke at 8:00am without benefit of any alarm clock. Gary decided he needed to go to the gym then find a coffee; I decided I needed a bath. At this time I mention what became a regular occurrence with my good friend. He enjoys a couple of cups of coffee in the morning when he gets up and I had noticed with shock that he would use both of the complimentary packets of coffee to make himself a pot. He would always graciously leave me the decaffeinated packets. In fairness he had asked one morning in Toronto if I wanted a cup and I had said I didn't which apparently precluded any need for him to ask again for the balance of the trip.

When Gary returned from his exercise we went down to the coffee bar for something to eat. While reading the papers we learned there had been six murders in Kansas City overnight, not six separate incidents mind. There had been two multiple murders so only four incidents if there was any solace to be taken from that. But anyway you put it six dead overnight seemed a lot.

The weather looked to be windy and cloudy and the paper suggested a high of 65F, or in my world 18C. A nice day for wandering about and in the lounge we fired up the Playbook for some research on what to do in Kansas City. We quickly discerned that we were in Missouri and that Kansas was across the river. We never discovered an explanation to the obvious question. After planning a course of action we headed back to the room to pick up cameras, jackets and the like. While awaiting on Gary brushing his teeth I watched a news segment on Veterans Day activities which we call Remembrance Day. The segment had people recalling where they were on 9/11.

KANSAS CITY OUT THE HOTEL WINDOW, LIKE REGINA YOU CAN WATCH YOUR DOG RUN AWAY FROM HOME FOR A WEEK

I have a vivid memory of my experience on that dreadful day. I was working and on a flight from Winnipeg to Thunder Bay that morning. The 50 minute trip was completely routine or so it seemed. When we landed the flight attendant advised there would be a delay in deplaning which started all sorts of chatter amongst passengers. While a handful of us were getting off, the balance were heading on to Toronto and were likely on business so probably had tight schedules. Five minutes later another announcement stated the pilot required everyone to deplane immediately. That started a lot of grumbling about lousy airline customer service, shoddy treatment and that sort of thing. At this point no one knew the reason.

Thunder Bay Airport, while not an international airport, was a new and up to date facility but without televisions for travelers to watch as in some other airports. There was a buzz in the waiting room - something had clearly happened. I was really in no rush and my normal routine in Thunder Bay was to check into the nearby Valhalla Hotel then cross the street to the rental car outlet. So I just blithely picked up my bags from the carousel and wandered through the unusually heavy crowd to a display board where local hotels advertise and used the courtesy phone to call the hotel and request the shuttle. The hotel is in view of the airport so it only ever takes a few minutes for the van to arrive.

The airport was quite crowded but it never crossed my mind that anything was terribly amiss. I just considered the crowds were the unlucky passengers from my flight and I just wanted to be on my way. The shuttle arrived and a couple of us got on and we headed out into the beautiful sunny morning. I did notice there were an unusual number of airplanes on the tarmac including a couple of big airplanes that you don't usually see in Thunder Bay. The shuttle driver was a big happy go lucky fellow who had chauffeured me a dozen times over the years. He mentioned that there had been a plane crash in the States. I recall a sense of sorrow for those involved but it was just a normal day for me and I was itching to get to work. I checked in without incident and took my bags to my room where I unpacked shirts and suits to minimize wrinkles before heading out to pick up my rental car. As I was waiting on the elevator to take me down to the lobby I glanced out the window and again noticed the dozen airplanes over at the airport, it was unusual. I walked across the highway to pick up the car then headed out to the commercial banking unit to begin my working day. I arrived just before noon and the half dozen staff were in the board room watching the horrible footage that we have now seen hundreds of times.

The airplanes on the tarmac were of course the result of the grounding of air traffic in North America. I was one of very few lucky travelers that day since I had a hotel and rental car booked. Every hotel in town was full and any means of travel by anything other than private vehicle was soon completely booked up. A number of people were forced to stay in the airport for a couple of days. I was also fortunate enough to have booked my trip for my usual four day visit. This would mean that all backlogged flights would be cleared up by time I headed home. I was not put out at all during those terrible few days. In hindsight it was a strange happenstance of circumstances.

Back in Kansas City and after getting everything needed for the day we were soon on our way. A different reception clerk suggested that the Liberty Memorial and National World War I Museum and the Kansas City Farmer's Market would both be good places to visit. The museum was within walking distance and situated on a small hill in Penn Valley Park directly opposite Union Station. We walked over in less than five minutes. You'll recall we spent half the previous night circumnavigating the globe in overhead walkways searching out the hotel.

The Kansas City area lost 400 soldiers in the Great War and while sad it was not truly a large number for a city of that size but the citizens took it to heart. Shortly after the war ended in 1918 a movement began in Kansas and Missouri to build a memorial to "the War to End all Wars" as a remembrance to those who gave the ultimate sacrifice and all veterans of the conflict. The city council appointed 40 prominent citizens to a memorial association to look into funding and in less than a year 83,000 contributors had raised more than $2.5 million, which in today's dollars would be more that $350 million. Ground was broken November 1, 1921 and the dedication ceremony took place November 11, 1926. Dignitaries in attendance included American President Coolidge, Lieutenant General Baron Jacques of Belgium, Admiral Beatty of the UK, General Diaz of Italy, Marshal Foch of France and U.S. General Pershing. In 1935 bas reliefs of the latter five were unveiled on a walkway wall. The site was created a National Historic Landmark on September 21, 2006 and is the official World War I museum of the United States.

It is an inspiring complex constructed with a limestone clad exterior in classical Egyptian Revival style. Local Bedford and Kasota granite stone, Italian travertine as well as terrazzo marbles were all utilized in its construction. There are huge bronze doors at the entranceway and the beacon at the peak of the 76 metre-high tower has orange lights to replicate a burning fire; its light can be seen for some distance.

The site tells the story of the 1914 to 1918 war utilizing two theatres, interactive displays, replica trenches and a large research and library centre. There's a large interior bridge from the entrance hall to the museum itself and beneath the glass floor of the bridge is a re-creation of a battle scarred field with 9,000 artificial poppy blooms each representing 1,000 people killed. The entire experience was quite sobering, the thought of all the dead made you stop. But have we really learned anything?

After viewing the interior space we went up and out onto the roof of the museum to access the tower itself. There was a small elevator just big enough for four people and I don't like small open cage elevators so had to steel myself. The operator sends you up from the bottom and when you wish to come back down you ring a bell. There was a circular staircase but it was closed for safety reasons, not that I would have considered using it. The view from the top was spectacular and you could see for miles.

The military seems everywhere in the U.S. and Americans have a great deal of pride in their military machine and its great strength and perceived successes. Yet some view that not every military adventure the Americans have undertaken during the past 50 years has been morally successful. One might also wonder that if even a small portion of the munitions they have rained down on others over the past half century had ever been deposited on U.S. soil would they still be so hawkish? It is all very well to protect the world from perceived evils but do we really know of the consequences of such overpowering force until such time as our own towns and countryside have been bombed flat and back to the Stone Age. War is not a video game.

After getting sorted out (we were always sorting ourselves out) we grabbed a cab to the City Market where we intended to get lunch and spend the afternoon wandering. We noticed for what wouldn't be the first time that cabs were very inexpensive compared to our respective home towns; I'd say nearly half the price. We would always ask someone to order us a cab, whether hotel, shop or restaurant clerk and no matter the city the request to call a cab was met graciously and the wait seldom longer than 15 minutes. This was not the experience where we come from. Interestingly, we seldom saw taxi stands with the exception of outside our hotel in Kansas City and at train stations.

We lunched on pizza and beer at a joint called Minsky's Pizza on the periphery of the City Market. We briefly considered sharing a pizza but ended up ordering our own. I am a traditionalist and require pepperoni with perhaps extra cheese while Gary, like my Lynn, daughters and so many other people have embraced so-called "gourmet" pizzas covered in chicken, pesto, goat cheese, dandelions and the like. We dined in the restaurant's small sun room attached to the front of the place, as the inside bar and restaurant were packed with people eating, drinking and watching football games on a dozen televisions. Amazingly there were numerous families with very young children enjoying the inside atmosphere. If you took young kids to such a place in Winnipeg you would risk losing them to Child and Family Services.

After lunch we checked out the market in the centre courtyard. It covered a couple of city blocks with all sorts of open air stalls. It was a nice sort of place as such places go but as we had little interest in food stuffs or handcrafted items we were through it in a relatively short time. We did, however, come across something I had never seen before - brussel sprouts on the stalk. I have always enjoyed sprouts but had no idea about how they grew. That they grow on a thick stalk nearly a metre high with sprouts "sprouting" out all round and over the stalk like some sort of weird alien life form took me completely by surprise.

Facing in on the central court, the Arabia Steamboat Museum was a Kansas City recommended destination. We walked in, bought tickets and were pleasantly surprised to learn that guided tours were running every half hour with the next one in 10 minutes. It turned out that we were visiting during the 20th anniversary of the museum. As a bonus, there was to be a screening of a seven minute film on the discovery of the boat and the development of the private museum with one of the discoverers scheduled to give a short talk.

In the 1850s the Missouri River played an important role in the transportation of people and tons of cargo to great swaths of the American west. The Missouri, then as now, was a wide, fast running and shallow river that constantly created new channels by the erosion of its banks. This erosion created navigational hazards of snags of floating trees and shifting sand banks. Most dangerous of all hazards were tree trunks that lodged in the bottom of the river, shorn of their branches by the fast-moving current and pointed like spears just below the surface and pointing into the current. The river was so treacherous that to this day people make a living as river pilots guiding boats up and down the waterway. The most famous river pilot to ply these waters was author Samuel Clemens, aka Mark Twain. His pseudonym was taken from the term shouted out from the bows of riverboats to indicate a depth of six feet of water was beneath the keel and so it was safe to proceed.

On September 6, 1856, the Kansas City Enterprise newspaper headline read:

Arabia Sunk
The steamer Arabia bound for Council Bluffs
struck a snag about a mile
below Parkville and sunk to the boiler deck
Boat and cargo a total loss

The *Arabia* had run into a snag head in the middle of the river and sunk in minutes. All passengers were saved but all cargo was lost. The fast-moving current quickly stripped the superstructure off the boat and the cargo on deck was washed into the river. The hull quickly sank into the mud of the river bottom and was soon completely covered by silt. At the time it was rumoured that there were great riches on board and many ill-fated attempts at salvage were undertaken over the years but to no avail. The *Arabia* quickly became a legend and for more than a century it remained lost to salvage. The course of the Missouri River was to be greatly altered over the next 150 years by the U.S. Corps of Engineers who ultimately built 45 dams to try and control the oft-time raging torrent.

In 1998 a number of friends banded together and decided to go treasure hunting. While the river had changed course quite a bit over the years many people still seemed to have a good idea where the wreck was resting - in the middle of a Kansas farm field nearly a kilometre from the present river course. What they didn't know was that it lay 14 metres beneath the field. It was a wonder they could find it at all. That fall the farmer who knew the *Arabia* lay buried under his land gave permission for an excavation. His permission was contingent on his field being ready for seeding the next spring. Amazingly in that short time period the ship was located, earth moved, artifacts and portions of the boat removed and all the dirt and more put back so the farmer could plant his crop in the spring. We all know that if this work had been undertaken by government agencies there would be little doubt that it would not have been accomplished in that time period nor on any schedule agreed to. During the course of this extraordinary feat the undertaking went from a treasure hunt for profit to a legacy for the people of Missouri.

A museum was built and restoration of the artifacts began. Today that restoration continues. There was little in the way of real treasure but what was found was the equivalent of a large department store worth of goods; imagine a Walmart store of the 1850s. There was everything you would want and could buy at general stores anywhere in the West and all of it brand new. Clothes, footwear, luxuries, food stuffs, wine, dishware, hardware, still full pickle jars and whiskey bottles. It had all been preserved by the silt of the Missouri River and was recovered in such in remarkable condition that it could readily be restored. The museum exhibits millions of pieces including thousands of pieces of dishware that had never had a knife and fork banging off them. They also recovered the portion of the Arabia's bow with the offending snag still stuck through the timbers of the hull. It is something to see.

Part of the admission price was a sliver of wood from the hull in a small glass bottle; at least they claim it was part of the hull.

The museum reminded me of my own riverboat wreck experience. In the quarter century prior to the 1860's, before the railway came through, riverboats used to come north up the Red River from St. Paul, Minnesota to Winnipeg bearing traffic and cargo. About 25 years ago when the Red was at one of its lowest levels in generations in Winnipeg, the burned-out hull of a St. Paul riverboat appeared out of the water at an old pier in a modern park just north of the city. My mum, Erin and I went out on a cold fall day for a look and along with a couple of dozen others walked about the remains of the hull looking for artifacts. I picked up a couple of bolts that have rested since at the bottom of a box in my garage along with some petrified dinosaur bones I found on another adventure.

After our tour of the museum we went back to Minsky's and our waitress graciously called us a cab. It was a beautiful day so we sat outside on a bench awaiting our ride. Whilst sitting there a guy from the bar with a full cast on his broken leg came outside for a smoke and struck up a conversation. Or rather, he started talking nonstop for 20 minutes. He soon learned we were from Canada and, unlike our pregnant hotel desk clerk, he had a pretty good idea where Winnipeg and Thunder Bay were. Our new friend knew Bob Dylan's home town of Hibbing, Minnesota was close by both of us, and then out of nowhere said that he loved Montreal. He gave us all sorts of advice on what to do and where to go in Kansas City.

As our cab drove off he was still babbling as he clomped along the sidewalk trying to keep up as he hurled suggestions at us.

On the way back to the hotel we asked the driver to stop so we could pick up a few things. We were running short of brandy and beer so he stopped at a gas station convenience store. Where else would one stop for liquor?

A little more than an hour and a half later we were at Union Station to meet up with Dave and Kathy for our steak dinner at the Piedmont Restaurant. We knew Kansas City was famous for beef, so stopping for a steak dinner had been our main and quite frivolous reason for visiting here. Like Buffalo wings in Buffalo the meal itself would be somewhat of a disappointment. The restaurant was pretty snazzy and completely full but the steak was just okay although I am not sure what I expected of a Kansas City steak. The company though was terrific and it turned out our dining companions had driven nearly an hour to meet us. They were better people than I. I'm afraid it would be a frosty Friday before I would drive 100 miles to dine with someone I had never met. Our new friends had never been to Canada and in fact Kathy had never been outside the U.S. While we did meet some well-travelled people we were regularly surprised by the number we'd met who had never left the U.S. While many said that they would like to travel most had never even had a passport. This is so uncommon to our Canadian experience where most people can't wait to get one.

(Later after the trip I learned that only 30% of Americans have a passport, which seems a phenomenally small number. The United States is considered a world power - if not the world power - and yet it appears its citizens don't explore the world, odd that.)

After such a big meal and a couple of drinks I fell asleep stuffed like a Christmas goose. I did wake up in the middle of the night with a cough and a sore throat. It persisted for an hour or so and I was worried that it would turn into something but as quick as it came it went.

November 13, Sunday – heading for Albuquerque, New Mexico back on The Lakeshore Limited

The day broke clear and blue with an expected high of 13C. I had phoned Lynn first thing and she seemed reasonably happy to hear from me. During the night Gary had shouted out Salinas in his sleep then rolled over and went back to sleep. It of course woke me up and I spent a little time humming *Me and Bobbi McGee*. We would be travelling through Salinas and I wondered if Gary's subconscious was going in the same direction. There were a great many places we would pass through that were mentioned in the songs and movies of my life:

Niagara Falls - a Marilyn Munroe movie
Buffalo - as in "shuffle off to ...."
Cleveland - Ian Hunter singing *Cleveland Rocks* later made famous again as the theme to Drew Carey's show
Toledo - as in "Holy ...."
Chicago - "That toddlin' town"
Kansas City - Ray Charles singing *Kansas City* here I come
Topeka - the site of numerous cowboy movies
Dodge City - Matt Dillon, the sheriff not the actor
Albuquerque - one of my favourite Neil Young tunes
Winslow - the Eagles hit (and one of Neil's favourites) song *Take it Easy*
Needles - Snoopy's brother's home
Anaheim - The Mighty Ducks
Santa Ana - the winds
San Juan Capistrano - swallows returning
San Clemente - Richard (I am not a crook) Nixon, better he should have been a crook than what he turned out to be
Los Angeles - *Dragnet*
Salinas - Kristofferson and Janis Joplin singing *Me and Bobbi McGee*
San Jose - Dionne Warwick singing *Do you know the way...*

With our train departure set for 10:45 pm and our hotel check out time 11:00am, we considered being at the station by 8:00pm would make for a reasonable wait. We were still thinking along the lines of protracted airport check-in times at this stage of the trip. You know, get to the airport two hours prior to a one-hour flight. There appeared to be a fairly long stretch pending, and contrary to our mutual thriftiness we decided that a late checkout would be of benefit. So while Gary was again exercising it fell to me to suck up to the desk clerk and see about the cheapest option for the latest possible check out time. We had agreed with no information forthcoming whatsoever that an additional cost of $30 to $40 each seemed a reasonable tariff. The plan would be to utilize the room until whatever time we could and then check our bags while we wandered about killing time.

When I went down to the front desk the same daft pregnant clerk was holding down the fort. She was again very inquisitive about Canada and where our train was headed. This interest notwithstanding she clearly had limitations regarding knowledge of her role within the hotel. She quickly offered up a 50% discount on the room rate for a late checkout but did not specify what time we needed to be out, a mistake and problem that I should have seen coming. I mentioned 8:00pm and she had seemed to suggest that would be fine.

I gave Gary the good news when back in the room and he rightly jumped on the obvious omission so went down to clarify. This was my second error in the process. I should have gone back as there was some consternation when Gary arrived at the front desk. He was dealing with another clerk who I might add had a handle on her role and duties. Gary had originally booked the room online via Expedia, which had provided a 50% discount on the room rate. The gracious 50% reduction offered by my clerk was based on the normal tariff for the room and not on what we were paying. Gary's much more clever clerk wanted to know who gave us the quote for the late checkout and Gary called up in a mild panic. The potential for any uncontrolled outflow of money always elicits a minor panic in both of us. Thirty years of slave wages and a natural inbred fear of spending were to blame for such stress. Anyway, when the pregnant girl was mentioned there was apparently a knowing sigh with eyes cast heavenward. The matter was referred to the manager, who agreed to a slightly more modest discount and a checkout time of 6:00pm. At first blush this seemed just mean spirited, I mean a deal's a deal. But we learned not only had the pregnant girl not understood the pricing issue, she had also overlooked that cleaning staff shift times impacted late checkouts. Six o'clock meant the room could be cleaned that day while any later meant it would not be done until the next. The hotel was booked solid and they needed the room.

We were reasonably happy with the revised offer as it meant we had the room for the balance of the day and could come and go as we pleased. The levy was to be $100 and while free would have been better, there you are. We convinced ourselves that a takeout lunch eaten in the room would offset some of the cost. This was the first real evidence I had of a weakening of the lock on Gary's wallet, and from this point he was to be somewhat freer with his cash. Which of course meant I had to be as well, damn his eyes. We are both pennywise at the best of times but to be honest I was prepared to throw a little money around and it may have started to rub off on my old friend.

With the long stretch in Depew still a sour memory I felt as though we now had a whole day to kill awaiting the night train. This was stupid and totally irrational thinking on my part. I should have been looking forward to the day rather than the night. Clearly I was not yet fully into the trip and was focusing on waiting on the night train rather than enjoying the opportunity at hand. Here I was in Kansas City, where I'd never been before and chances are would never be again, and instead of a plan to see more of the city I was just jerking around trying to figure out a way to kill some time. Later that night when I realized what a shame it was to not have taken better advantage of the day I resolved to try and ensure it didn't happen again. I think we succeeded reasonably well.

We needed a drink after the minor imbroglio so we took the opportunity and sat down in the lounge on the second floor walkway, one of those that had collapsed all those years ago. We wanted to update our emails and the lounge seemed to have the clearest wifi signal at the moment. I discovered a message from Neil offering a week at their holiday home in Hawaii. He was going to be dropping us off at the Portland Airport after our visit and then travel on to Hawaii that same morning and he wanted to know I wished to spend a week there. It was a wonderful offer but I had appointments at home that I foolishly felt I could not rearrange from the U.S. This would turn out to be my day for stupid mistakes. I had the phone numbers and could have made it happen and I came to deeply regret the decision.

While sitting in the lounge, Gary working his emails and me reading the paper, four women walked by and one asked how we had enjoyed our meal the night before. In hindsight they likely thought we were part of some convention in the place, possibly even their own. We were both gob smacked since unknown women speaking to us had not been a common occurrence for either of us for some many years. In fact for one of us it was quite a novel experience. Perhaps American women are more forward. Our shock must have been apparent as one of them immediately mentioned they had seen us in the Piedmont Restaurant. We said that we had enjoyed the meal which was really not quite accurate but we'd had to think fast and string together some sort of response. I would like to say that they were four hot chicks, but they were likely our age with not a looker in the bunch. Of course we both considered that since they had seen, remembered and approached us we clearly still 'had it.' (Frankly I had never been aware of ever having 'it.') We undoubtedly misconstrued a friendly conversation from one group towards another but nevertheless it made our day.

Gary was of the opinion they approached us because of our rock star looks. He believed his completely hairless head and my overabundance of hair coupled with my Gretsch Guitar T-shirt were positively working for us. I told him I doubted his rationale completely and then went off on a tangent detailing my lifelong fear of barbers and hair cutting in general due to traumatic teenage experiences with a mother who spent 10 years practicing but never quite perfecting hair cutting on her children. Mum used one of those comb things with a razor blade attached that were advertized on television to be the greatest thing since sliced bread. They weren't. The damn things tended to chop and hack rather than neatly trim. It was possible a newish blade might have made a difference but there wasn't much money in those days so my brother and I had to endure dire threats to our wellbeing if we "didn't damn well sit still."

And then another of the now seemingly never-ending reminders of home occurred. When I went back to the papers after the strange women incident an article in the Kansas City Star caught my eye. It was about the rollout of the new television season in Los Angeles and the local scribe mentioned his colleague Brad Oswald of the *Winnipeg Free Press*. I was finding you never had to look hard to find connections.

After all the morning's excitement had died down we started to make plans. Gary had brought a book to read that he found to be intolerable and I had broken a brush that morning so we figured we could do some shopping. Off we went and quickly discovered great masses of humanity wandering about the lobby of the hotel - and it was one big lobby. The conventions the hotel had been catering to were over and they were disgorging guests out of the place. There were people moving about everywhere like rats leaving a sinking ship. It looked to be nice and sunny out so discretion being the better part of valour we chose to run from the crowds and head outdoors.

It turned out that there was not much happening in that part of outdoor Kansas City on a Sunday morning.

While we were out walking I found it odd not to see bilingual English and French instructions on street signs and for the first time I noticed people had an accent, sort of a soft "you all" type of thing. The mall shops we were headed for didn't open until noon and as we were a few minutes early we opted for a coffee in a small food court which had enormous two storey glass front windows. While chatting I noticed a huge black airplane coming in for a landing. It was gigantic and moving slowly and quietly like a surreal movie dream sequence. There were a few people in the place but none of them seemed to notice but us. It was so big it seemed to block out the sun and its shadow preceded it as it flew over. It was a Stealth bomber preparing to land at a nearby military base. The size of the airplane and the lack of noise was quite startling.

The sight brought back memories of an air show nearly 40 years ago when I watched a British Vulcan bomber fly overhead in a similar manner with a similar shadow, but that time the noise had been deafening. That memory started a conversation of airplanes seen and ridden on. I recounted the tale of Lynn and I returning home from England on a 747 when we were stopped on the access road to the runway as the last flight of the Concorde flew into Heathrow. I had a perfect view of the four planes looking like whopping cranes landing one after the other and then smartly lining up on the tarmac. I also had seen a new giant Airbus being tested at the Toulouse airport on a trip we'd taken to France and I seemed to recall flying over a static display of a Concorde on that same tarmac. It has always been fascinating to watch something so large gracefully fly through the air.

We wandered about the mall after our coffee to pass the time and checked out some restaurants for dinner but everything seemed to close up at 5:00pm. We were in Kansas City's business district and just like Winnipeg, it seems that after business hours the place shuts down. The old adage about rolling up the sidewalks sprang to mind.

We took lunch back to the hotel room and over that meal planned the next one for the hotel bar immediately after checking out.

Weather-wise it turned out to be a beautiful day, but we didn't really get much accomplished other than wandering around outside and sitting about the room. The day seemed to go by quickly enough though and by 6:00pm we had packed up, checked out and stored our bags on the way to the bar. I complimented my salad with a Michelob beer, a brand I hadn't had in 30 years. I wasn't really hungry after the takeout lunch sandwich but the beer tasted good. While supping the beer I seemed to recall that Eric Clapton enjoyed Michelob beer or at least said in paid advertisements that he liked the stuff. The bar was completely full and yet no one seemed to be distracted or even remotely bothered by an enormous black flying bug that was buzzing each and every table in sequence. Over the course of the meal our waitress had told us that the hotel would be soon changing over to a Sheraton after 31 years as a Hyatt.

After stretching out dinner as long as humanly possible we went back for our bags at half past seven. While a bell boy was retrieving our bags from the bowels of the cloakroom his partner provided additional information on the pending changes to the hotel. He had little loyalty left to his employer since he was not going to be a part of the change. We learned that the Hall family of Hallmark card fame had their fingers on much of the economic pulse of Kansas City. It seemed they'd had some difficulty with the Hyatt chain; the Halls' apparently do not put up with difficulties so they were switching brands. The rumour was that Sheraton would be undertaking $18 million in renovations. Difficulty with partners is bound to happen over time but an $18 million sweetener would likely help make any decision to switch partners much easier. Conversation completed and bags collected we sauntered over to the station. This time we walked outside avoiding the overhead walkway system. We weren't in much of a hurry and it was the wrong approach to kill time. The walk took 10 minutes rather than the interminable half a lifetime of our first evening.

When we arrived we found the train station waiting room was not much bigger than the one in Buffalo-Depew and this small space allocated to the railway was only a tenth of the grand old Union Station. They had kept some of the old waiting room benches and they were quite similar in design to church pews.

Funny that church pews are also running out of bums to sit upon them and I wondered if there was a connection. There were just less than a dozen folks waiting on our train, we knew they were likely going with us since there wasn't another train til the early hours of the morning. One of the waiting passengers was stretched out snoozing quite noisily. I have regularly been told I snore quite raucously and as a result I have always been quite aware of not falling asleep in public. The guy on the bench would have been well served by such a personal policy.

We were of course at the station hours before departure which inevitably required Gary to check the departure board a number of times. The funny thing about posted railway departure boards is that they never seem to change. If the train was scheduled to arrive at 11:00am the notice board would read and remain 11:00am. Even if those in charge knew it was going to be late - even by hours - they would not change the notice board. It does make a twisted sort of sense. If you call before you leave home you will be told the expected arrival and departure time. If you're foolish enough to arrive without first calling you will be sitting there when they make announcements or, if you are like Gary, get up and check with the train agent halfway between each announcement. Why go to the bother and work of changing a sign when there is no need especially if the train is scheduled to arrive and depart daily at the same time. Leaving the board alone and dealing with the captive market's demands for information when presented seems like a reasonable approach when you considered it.

I read a little bit and wrote a little bit and time passed pleasantly enough. I was finally learning when you have no control it is best to just let it go and enjoy where you are.

Kansas City to Albuquerque

The train arrived on time at 10:10pm and disgorged dozens of passengers. We were scheduled to depart 40 minutes later and were quickly hustled on board. In no time at all we were comfortably ensconced in our compartment which was already set up for sleeping. After a quick brandy or two I took the upper berth and this time there was no window and I made a mental note to have a wee chat with Gary. There would be no upper berth windows for the balance of the trip (a bad thing) but there no longer toilets in the compartments (a good thing).

November 14, Monday

Up at 7:00am and after trying to wash and deal with other more personal tasks whilst bouncing like a super ball off the bathroom walls I was ready for tea and breakfast. It was a pretty impressive breakfast: eggs, sausage, potatoes, grits (if wanted - they weren't), toast and a bit of fruit. Normally it would have been too much for me but it was included in the price of the ticket so I ate it all. A side consideration was that we had spent a lot of money on meals in Kansas City and we were of the opinion that we should eat as much free food as we could sink our teeth into. There again seemed to be no time pressure on us during breakfast so we enjoyed the meal as the world rolled by the window. We passed through Granada, Kansas as we ate.

Our breakfast companion was a veterinarian named Stephen and naturally Gary got the conversation going. Stephen had grown up in Dodge City and came from a family of vets but he'd moved 30 years ago to Los Angeles for the outdoor lifestyle which I took to mean the ocean. He told us he returned home regularly and always travelled back and forth by train. We had apparently stopped in Dodge City an hour before I got up and while I did recall the stop I did not realize it had been "Dodge City". If I had I might have stepped onto the platform. Isn't there and old saying about "getting out of Dodge"? Gary somehow moved the conversation around to money and by the end of breakfast Stephen suggested that recompense for veterinarians seemed much higher in Canada.

You always seem to talk weather with new people and we did. We learned there was a terrible drought going on which was obvious from the dry brown fields and the many half-empty ponds. Everything was parched except for the grain fields. They were being irrigated by the same type of irrigation contraptions that irrigate potato fields in Manitoba, long pipes spaced between gigantic bicycle-like wheels. We never see wheat field irrigation at home and it must be a brutally expensive way to farm.

By 9:15am we were getting close to the Colorado state line with La Junta just half an hour away. I have recently seen a 1952 film noir detective movie set on a train on this same rail line. In one scene the hero stepped down from the train at La Junta, the station has not changed in 60 years. The landscape was starting to look different and another time zone was pending. The land had been pretty flat since we left Chicago but we were now getting close to our first views of mountains.

When we returned from breakfast our compartment had been magically transformed back to armchairs and we spent a little time reading, talking and writing. Gary used his Playbook to record his thoughts while I scribbled in my journal. After about an hour and a half we sauntered down to the observation car for a change of scenery. Walking down the passageway of sleeping cars can be tricky even without people coming at you from the other direction. The passage was about 60 cm wide and any sway of the carriage could quite easily put you off balance. If you were off balance it was easily and quickly arrested by your bouncing back and forth off the walls, unless of course somebody's compartment door was open, in which case you ran a good chance of ending up on somebody's lap. The toughest part of walking through the train, however, was always the transition between carriages. The joining point was always completely enclosed with no sight of any sort of the mechanical connections but this was always the point where the sideways motion of the train seemed the greatest. I sometimes leapt into the adjoining carriage and felt sorry for older passengers as it could be a real challenge especially when there was a line-up to get a seat in the dining car. During such line-ups people could find themselves trapped in the transition zone for a couple of minutes.

The Amtrak observation cars did not have a bubble top like Canadian trains but they still afforded terrific views out both sides and from windows set high on the walls that curved up into the ceiling. The cars had big comfortable armchairs in various configurations, side by side and facing each other in groupings of two and four. We spent some time there as the Rockies slowly came into view. Later in what I assumed were foothills a little bit of snow started to appear on the ground in gullies and the shade afforded by evergreen trees. It seemed like they were the first trees we'd seen in some time.

Since it was by now getting close to lunchtime and as we had books and the tablet with us we ventured back to our compartment to drop stuff off. While there I noticed that the front of the rubber sole on my right shoe was sporting a gaping hole. Nothing lasts anymore! I had only been wearing those shoes regularly for 10 years and here they were worn out already. When getting ready for the trip I had spent weeks trying to decide which shoes to bring and had struggled between walking shoes for an urban setting or a more utilitarian hiking boot. I finally decided on the walking shoes and now they had let me down. I had also brought sandals but who knew if they were going to be of any use except in San Diego. Something would need to be done about my shoes and fast. Between Gary's less than compassionate belly laughs I struggled to figure out a fix rather than having to buy new shoes. Happily for Gary my dilemma would provide countless moments of mirth for the balance of the trip.

The tracks took us through only a small portion of south eastern Colorado and just before 11:00am we entered New Mexico at Raton. At 7,900 feet above sea level this was the highest elevation we would reach on the trip, (notwithstanding airplane rides of course) and it was to be all downhill from here, literally, not figuratively. There was a lot of snow now and the railway information pamphlet told us we were on the legendary Santa Fe Trail. In the days before the railway it must have been a heck of a hike. Our train had been under a real load on the way to the crest near Raton but now on the other side of the peak you could feel it moving freer as we started down. The scenery was spectacular and the train switched back on its self quite often; sometimes you could see the front of the train sometimes the back. It was beautiful country.

We were soon travelling through the high plains which were amazingly all fenced to keep cattle in. It was something to be so far from civilization with all the land fenced off and not a road in sight. We did see a couple dozen elk in a pasture that was home to a herd of cattle but I guessed they couldn't be charged with trespassing. The sky went on forever and what with mountains in the background, the foothills and the plains I expected Clint Eastwood to come riding over the horizon on his appaloosa. As we finished lunch we passed through Las Vegas, New Mexico, not to be confused with the other one in Nevada. Our schedule "suggested" we should have been about three hours from Albuquerque and our second stopping off point.

THE HIGH PLAINS OF NEW MEXICO

We had enjoyed lunch with an older couple from Niles, Michigan who were on their way to Los Angeles to visit a daughter. I continued to find connections to home and they couldn't be coincidence as they were happening all the time. I had by now come to the opinion that everyone on earth was connected and you just had to take the time to determine how. This couple knew of both Winnipeg and Thunder Bay by way of his brother marrying a Regina woman in 1962 and the couple's subsequent relocation there. Our new friends had travelled through both of our home towns during various family visits to Regina over the years. Our lunch mate was a Lutheran pastor and Gary is a Lutheran and I being an Anglican am now liked within the Lutheran Church, in Canada at least. They told us they had done relief work in the Red River Valley of North Dakota during the 1997 'flood of the century' which had also caused a great deal of strive in Winnipeg. They had also spent five months doing relief work in New Orleans after Katrina. Their life of selfless service was quite eye opening for us.

It was about this time I found I needed my glasses all the time. I had been kidding myself that I only need them to read. The truth is I can barely read my watch without them. Gary had a laugh and would continue to bring up that I had not brought my new glasses on the trip just in case something happened to them.

That they were also a new stronger prescription only added to his good humour. All this contributed to my deciding to wear them more and it was a good thing I wised up as the vistas were now truly spectacular.

The soil and rock outcrops were a fiery red and there were huge channels cut in the plains eroded by water over the millennium. Many of the channels were 10 or more metres deep and twice that across and they ran for miles off into the distance. In one spot where a small creek was running at the bottom of a gully six cars had been pushed off the bank. They were placed so neatly that I hoped they had been put there to stop erosion from flash flooding rather than just pushed over at a convenient spot. There were also strange round trees dotting the landscape like freckles on a red-headed kid's face, but no green anywhere.

We were starting to get back into civilization and as we had seen throughout the journey the more depressed areas of human habitation tended to be around the railway line. It made perfect sense. The first settlers would have built close to the transportation line and as they prospered they moved away with new groups of less fortunates moving in. The houses and ever-increasing number of house trailers tended to be on the rundown side with each invariably home to a backyard populated by abandoned cars and pickup trucks that were sinking into the earth. I have a 1951 Chevrolet pickup that I continually invest blood, sweat and tears of frustration in to keep it running down the road. I was to see dozens of them out the train window and such a close proximity to hard-to-get rust-free parts was maddening.

While travelling past a herd of cattle we noticed a dead one on the ground away from the herd. I wondered how long it had been there and how it would be disposed of. From our vantage point it appeared we were miles from anywhere but of course there could have been a city out of sight just over the next hill or at the very least the ranch house of the owner.

We had now been travelling downhill for some time and were low enough that there was no longer any snow about and the types of trees had changed. There were fewer evergreens and the new types had all lost their leaves. It reminded me of home in late October with sunny but crisp air. All the land was still fenced and it was hard to fathom that anyone could own so much. The need to post ever-increasing numbers of No Trespassing signs seemed like a needless affront from the train window. There were no signs of people for miles on end so who would be in a position to trespass or read the signs if they were thinking about trespassing?

Just before 3:00pm there was an announcement over the intercom that some sort of signal issue had occurred and we were being delayed. This was not much of a surprise really as the train had been stopping and going off and on for over an hour and we barely crept along when we were moving. We knew something was amiss and were told to expect to be an hour and a half late into Albuquerque. That would be train time of course and by 6:00pm we were still an hour from our destination. Happily they had called us to dine early because of the delay. We were not expecting to have dinner on the train so this was a free meal and there was nothing wrong with that.

As usual we'd been seated with another traveler for dinner. Now up to this point all fellow diners had been gracious and friendly and from this point on they would also be, but not this fellow this night. Our dining companion was the surliest and most unpleasant person I have ever had the misfortune of sitting across from and that was quite an accomplishment. I spent over three decades working in a bank where I discovered that a customer's surliness and unpleasantness usually had a direct relationship to dealing with their money or the lack thereof. I'd come across a lot of unpleasant people in my time but none had anything on this guy. He was well over six feet tall and was so hearty that the fixed table of the booth could not adequately accommodate his girth between the bench and the table. A goodly portion of him was pressed onto and over the table. Undoubtedly this made him uncomfortable and cranky, but still.

We said hello, to which he grudgingly responded with little more than a grunt. We tried to engage him in the normal pleasant platitudes but to no avail. Since we were on our way to Albuquerque I asked in all innocence if it was his home town thinking that this would not in any way be offensive nor prying. His response was a curt "no" without any additional information forthcoming. I am not as outgoing nor as friendly with new people as Gary and as a result of his curt response decided that this was not a person I had any desire or intention to communicate with further. I just tucked into my dinner ignoring the guy across the table and conversed with Gary throughout the rest of our meal. At the time I thought what a miserable SOB and if he wanted to be quietly on his own it was okay with me. Later that night I was ruminating on the bugger and thought that perhaps it might have been something we had done to upset him. The only thing that I could consider was that we had both ordered light dinners; I had opted for a salad in fact. He followed suit and I wondered if he had ordered salad out of shame. I know this might sound miserable and patronizing but he did devour the communal bowl of buns and his dessert with extreme gusto. It may have been that he didn't order what he wanted and so knew that the dinner wouldn't satisfy him. Anyway it was no loss as I have long since stopped worrying or caring about folks who choose not to be pleasant.

While we were dining the train crew discovered the brakes on the baggage car had seized and this added to the potential for further delays. We had noticed a funny odour during dinner which reminded me of a car's burnt clutch.

I knew about burnt clutches from my wayward youth. One day at seventeen I was showing off in my dad's 1961 Pontiac Laurentian when I revved the beejesus out of the engine, then, as they say, I "popped the clutch". It is an apt saying as the clutch did in fact pop, amidst a terrible burning smell. I made up some fanciful tale of unexplained mechanical failure which my dad, a machinist, accepted with a raised eyebrow. We replaced the clutch the next evening lying on our backs outside on the gravel driveway by the light of my mum's temporarily repurposed living room lamp. My dad is a clever man; I have not "popped" a clutch since.

We had been stopped dead throughout dinner and reports from the dining car staff suggested that the crew couldn't get the brakes to free up. Some of our fellow diners had started to voice concerns over the delay as many had connections to make at the end of the line in California. Happily we were completely unconcerned as we were getting off and staying in Albuquerque for a couple of days and we had just finished a free dinner.

At one point during the dinner all the power on the train was turned off as part of some attempt at a fix. We had our meals in front of us and the dining car had battery lighting so even this was of no concern to us. However, the rest of the train was making do with emergency lighting and as it was dark out people were getting ticked off. Passenger patience was getting to be in short supply and some people were trying to get into the dining car for nonexistent seats. A guy actually sneakily sat down thinking that nobody would notice, silly fellow. Staff were trained to note people who were not where they should be or more importantly where they shouldn't be.

There may have been trouble brewing for some but not for us sleeper car people. We were well looked after and dined with lights and in comfort. I felt no shame and while this may not say much for compassion for my fellow passengers, there you are.

Ultimately the crew placed a call to the Delaware headquarters and it was decided to proceed come hell or high water. The train must get through type of thinking, I guess. The plan was to creep to a nearby siding to figure out the next step. Clearly they couldn't have us sitting on the main line holding up trains on either side of us but it seemed likely to me that if the brakes were seized, moving to the nearest siding would only make them hot and could well fuse them to the wheels. Then there was a stroke of luck for the railway. While we had been sitting and the experts had been trying to figure out what to do the brakes had cooled off enough that they released themselves. To ensure no further problems the brakes on the baggage car were disconnected and we eventually reached our destination at 8:00pm.

We departed the train in Albuquerque and while I don't know what happened I'll bet they sat in the station for a further couple of hours while they sorted out the brakes on the baggage car. I am guessing anybody with a connection to make in Los Angeles likely missed it.

The Albuquerque train station was a modern building in the Old West design and looked like it could have been the setting of a detective movie from the 1940s. We walked through the small station and out into the New Mexico air, got into a cab and said "Holiday Inn Express Old Town." Twenty minutes later we were in our hotel room. We had a couple of brandies to calm our nerves, well actually just because they tasted good. We kicked back and watched television and caught up on email and even talked around some sort of an agenda for the next couple of days. We had originally planned to pick up a rental car directly from the station but they were closed by time we arrived so we would have to figure that out. Our thoughts had been to drive to Santa Fe to visit the Georgia O'Keefe Museum on our first day. The car rental place being closed was a shame really. Gary has an almost pathological hatred of Hyundai cars as a result of some sort of experience with their 1980s Pony model, and knowing this I had of course reserved a Hyundai.

November 15, Tuesday

We awoke around 7:00am and I noticed I was having trouble catching my breath. It was almost like a cold coming on but I was reasonably sure that the mile-high altitude had everything to do with it. I had read that the body soon gets used to thinner air but I am sure I never did adjust and it was a good thing I had no plans on running a marathon. On reflection my shortness of breath had everything to do with altitude and not the state of my physical fitness and that is the story I am going with. When each of our waking up in the morning stuff was completed we sauntered down to the common room for our free breakfast. We didn't have much in the way of expectations but they were exceeded. It was a big room at the front of the hotel with a dozen tables and we could see mountains through a wall of windows. There was a full selection of hot drinks and juice, an apparatus to make pancakes and of course different types of cereals and fruit. There was also a small buffet with muffins, sticky buns and hot plates of sausage, eggs, bacon, grits and a chipped beef concoction. Being traditionalists we opted to avoid grits as well as the chipped beef. Since we really had no idea when the eggs were cooked we also gave them a miss. But all in all it was a decent breakfast. After browsing through the papers we settled down to come up with a plan for the day and it transpired that neither of us was in any rush to get the rental car. In Kansas City we'd found that cabs were so cheap and easy to get that when we considered the aggravation of trying to find our way around a strange city, not driving was looking like a plus. But it would take us a couple of days and numerous discussions to finally make a decision around the rental.

We hadn't been away from home very long but getting access to laundry services was looming as a potential irritant. Something as simple as not being able to get access to such facilities either as a do it yourselfer or paying for the service can weigh on a person inclined to cleanliness. Happily it turned out the hotel had a washing machine and dryer on each floor that we decided to take advantage of later that evening. In my travels I have discovered that in-house laundry is not always a common situation. In England the problem was not access to a washer but that dryers are not as commonplace as they are in North America.

The hotel receptionist was quite helpful in giving us ideas on what to do and see. We had already decided to take the 10 minute cab ride to the Old Town as Dave, one of my oldest friends, had been here a couple of times and suggested that Old Town was a place we should visit. We were inclined to leg it over but were told it wasn't a nice walk as much of it was along a highway that didn't have sidewalks. We didn't easily give up on thoughts of walking but there were to be quite a number of people over the course of the visit who discouraged us from doing so, not for safety concerns but just because of the absence of sidewalks.

By 9:00am it was already a quite pleasant 13C and I decided to wear sandals and put off the issue of my walking shoes. First things being first and before the day could begin we, like the chicken, crossed the road. In our case it was to get to the Walgreens on the other side as we needed supplies.

When it came to replenishing supplies it primarily meant the need to refresh brandy stocks and happily Walgreens had a liquor store attached. Dave used to have a nonsensical response to an offer of a drink when I was younger - "a beer if it's near or a brandy if it's handy" - and happily both were near and handy at Walgreens. It was quite a well-stocked liquor outlet when you consider it was in a drug store and if you can believe it Gary was going to buy a Californian brandy. I hoped it was a misguided attempt at being price conscious and I did dissuade him fairly quickly and forcefully. Californian indeed; what were we, tourists?

I picked up a hair brush to replace the one I had broken and not replaced in Kansas City and also a packet of disposable razors. Even though I had packed and repacked at home a dozen times all the while checking off a list I had forgotten my shaving stuff. The hotel had offered up a convenience package of shaving cream and a disposable razor but the razor could barely scratch at my whiskers and I don't have a heavy beard.

It was there at Walgreens that I had a flash of genius around my shoe issue. Lightning had struck in aisle six. I would fix my shoes by filling up the hole with silicon glue. Gary was skeptical of my plan to say the least and the situation would continue to give him chuckles for some time to come. Secretly things were actually worse than Gary knew and I was loathe to tell him that my left shoe was showing signs of the same affliction as its mate.

Back at the hotel and prior to heading out to Old Town I put the fix on my shoes. I leaned both up against the closet door and squeezed my newly purchased clear glue into the holes at the front of the soles. The left shoe took very little but the opening on the right shoe seemed to be an access point to a bottomless pit. The task completed, we were on our way out the door to a chorus of Gary's snickering and guffaws and that made it personal. Buying a new pair of shoes was no longer even on the table. I would fix those damn shoes rather than buy a new pair just to shut him up. I was going to prove to Gary that the old motto of the Round Table: Adopt, Adapt and Improve would save the day. I am not exactly sure that it was in fact the motto of the Round Table but an old Monty Python movie said it was so.

We were finally off on the day's adventures in Old Town and it looked to be a great day for it. The cab ride was just $10, a bus would have been likely half of that and a rental car would have been close to $40 a day plus gas. So cabs seemed quite a reasonable approach but our pending decision around renting a car was still far from being finalized. Why we struggled so long to make a decision now seems foolish but struggle we did.

Old Town was the original colony of Albuquerque, established by the Spanish Governor of New Mexico in 1706 with 12 pioneering families. Amazingly, many of the buildings were original although they were all shops now and no personal residences remained. Being a Tuesday in the middle of November it was not overly crowded but everything was open. There was enough foot traffic to make it a pleasant wander and all the shopkeepers were very happy to see us. I was still feeling a little out of sorts and thought it might have been the shortness of breath or maybe it was the laughs Gary was enjoying at my expense or maybe it was a bit of undigested cheese from breakfast.

After about an hour of looking around we stopped for a mid-morning hot drink at a place called Bebe's Café. I always prefer whole milk in my tea, picky I know but cream or half and half makes the tea too thick and 2% milk makes it too thin and don't get me started on skim. Just to be contrary I do like evaporated milk in my tea but only at the cottage. I admit it makes the tea "thick" but at the lake this is not a bother for some reason. Anyway the café owner who I assumed to be the "Bebe" on the sign happily provided whole milk for my tea and said she had it on hand because she preferred it herself. What a retail concept, providing customers with the things you know and like despite a modest cost. Gary and I sat about for half an hour talking about nothing in particular but I do recall a conversation around motorcycles, bike jackets, riding in cold weather and my daughter Sara's recent purchase of a Honda 250. In hindsight this was an unusual conversation as I don't believe Gary ever had any interest in motor bikes. Strangely a few moments later while searching for a washroom I stumbled across a Honda that was the same model as Sara's. Reminders of home continued to be all about.

THE AUTHOR OUTSIDE BEBE'S

A COURTYARD IN OLD TOWN

Old Town turned out to be a shopping centre spread over half a dozen blocks laid out around a central square. Since Gary and I were not really shopping for anything once we had seen a dozen tourists shops selling everything that tourists are looking to buy we had pretty well seen everything there was to see, retail wise. So we took a tour of the San Felipede Nevi Church, which was the oldest building in Albuquerque. The church had been constructed of wood, straw and mud brick and was in remarkable condition which was undoubtedly a result of the dry climate. In the laneway directly behind the church was a restaurant that a half dozen people had told us we had to visit. We had been told the Casa De Ruiz Church Street Café served a great meal and we would always take advice offered around meals on this trip. We hadn't always done so on our England walk and we had lived (barely) to regret it. I had chicken tacos and Gary had a chicken taco salad washed down with a local beer for me and red wine for him. We ate on the outside patio which had once been the home's front garden.

SAN FELIPEDE NEVI CHURCH

    The Casa de Ruiz, the house of Ruiz, was built by one of the founding families in 1706 and was continuously owned and lived in by the Ruiz family until 91 year old Riafina G Ruiz died in 1991. The house was built out of handmade Terrones bricks crafted from the nearby Rio Grande river mud. The architecture of Old Town reminded me of what I had seen on visits to Mexico. The low roof lines and thick walls with stone tile floors helped keep rooms cool in the heat of the day.

    As usual we had barely finished lunch before Gary was deciding what to do for dinner. It amazes me that such a skinny guy who does not appreciate less than wholesome food and who would slit his throat before he would eat a jelly donut had such preoccupation with ensuring where his next meal was coming from. I have travelled with him enough that I barely notice planning dinner halfway through lunch anymore. We decided that a take-out meal in the hotel room would be in order. We had been running around most of the day and as we intended to utilize the laundry facilities eating in made some sense. Plus the spectre of having spent more than we expected on meals in Kansas City was still hanging above our heads.

Our waiter at lunch was covered in turquoise jewelry including a huge plate-sized silver ring that covered three of his fingers. He was a bit of a doufus and was unknowingly sporting a paper 'kick me' sign on the back of his shirt. In passing he recommended a local discount jewelry store where he claimed we would get the best deals on anything we were looking to buy and it was just a couple of blocks away. The directions seemed pretty clear and we had little else to do so off we went. The prices did seem more reasonable than the Old Town shops and as they were having a sale I bought each of my girls a turquoise necklace. Once this was done we considered we had given Old Town enough time and so asked a lady in a tourist centre to call us a cab for the ride back to our hotel.

Once back in the room our conversation inevitably turned to dinner. We had decided a meal in was on tap and so all that was to be decided upon was from whence it would come. Outside our second floor window to the left was the Walgreens and to its right across a road and directly opposite us was a strip mall with a gas bar with a large convenience store attached. The day before we had discovered when looking in that the store offered a large assortment of packaged sandwiches and the like. Built alongside the gas station was an Arby's fast food outlet that neither of us had much experience with other than television commercials that offered roast beef sandwiches as their claim to fame. Considering experiences in the past with packaged sandwiches, we figured Arby's would be a decent choice. So we walked across and picked up take away with Gary opting for chicken, at a place known for its roast beef. I stuck with the beef. We had bought a box of beer when we bought brandy that morning so we sat around supping our beer and eating dinner watching the news while washing machines and dryers completed their appointed tasks.

Over the course of the evening we kicked around plans for the next day including cabbing it to Nob Hill. This area was reputed to be a trendy and hip shopping area. We also discussed potential visits to museums and we were still waffling about the rental car, postponing that decision yet again. We left it at maybe picking it up at 4:00pm and then heading up to Santa Fe the following morning. But the writing was surely on the wall.

Before hitting the hay we checked our emails with spotty access once again. During the past couple of hotel stays we'd discovered that around meal times and late evening it was harder to get online access. It likely had everything to do with hotel guests all trying to get access at the same time. It turned out I didn't have any messages anyway.

November 16, Wednesday

It was nice to start the day with clean laundry. It is funny how such an innocuous issue at home can prey so heavily on one's thoughts when there's no ready access to a washing machine. The opportunity when presented is a big deal and should not be taken lightly.

At 9:00am it was sunny and 3C with an expected high of 14C - a perfect day for exploring. Gary had been online to see what was happening in Santa Fe in a last ditch effort at trying to make a final decision around the car. We both figured if we were going to drive an hour and a half to get there we should have some idea of what we wanted to do once we arrived. Whilst online researching Santa Fe he'd discovered that just across the road and down from the convenience/gas bar was the pueblo museum. It had earlier been highly recommended by a hotel receptionist but we hadn't acted on it because we weren't really sure where it was at the time. We decided to give it a go first thing and then visit an outdoor complex called the Albuquerque Bio Park which included gardens, a zoo and aquarium. We expected we would spend a goodly portion of the day at the park so Nob Hill could wait. Ever still waffling we thought we could pick up the rental car on the way back to the hotel late in the afternoon. If we could make a definitive decision that is. We were spending far too much time thinking about and putting off the issue of the rental car.

Before heading off we checked emails again and this time I had a few, including one from my Sara. My son-in-law Colin took up playing the bagpipes a few years back and has become quite proficient. If he wasn't my son-in-law I would make a crack about how could you possibly tell if someone was proficient at playing the pipes. My kids have an uncle who also plays the pipes and their mum's uncle, a cad, used to say bagpipes only sound good on a hill. A hill far, far away. Anyway, Colin had become proficient enough to have been asked to join the Winnipeg Police Band (he is a school teacher, not a member of the police force, if that means anything). Sara's message was that the band was playing at half time of the last game of the season of our Winnipeg Blue Bomber football team. The Bombers would continue on successfully through the finals and earn a spot at the Grey Cup Game which was to be played on the day Gary and I flew home. I was blissfully unaware of the Big Blue's semi final success and advancement to the big one until we arrived at the airport in Vancouver. Unfortunately they lost the final.

Colin's playing at the game reminded me of my dad's attempts to take up and play an instrument when I was in my late teens. In his 40s Dad had joined the Khartoum Temple Shrine and was soon in the Marching Fife and Drum Band where he tried hard to master the fife. I don't believe I am giving away any of the secret society's secrets in saying that when the band performed in parades or at the circus my dad would mimic playing. If he hadn't lip-synced the sounds that would have emanated from his fife would have been, to say politely, discordant. The major difference between Dad and Colin was that one could actually play but I have digressed once again.

A little background on the Indian Pueblo Cultural Centre Showcase would seem appropriate. The lifestyles, religion and arts of the 19 different pueblos of New Mexico were on display at the centre. There were numerous dioramas and exhibits of how people lived and played as well as cultural displays of art and the day to day trappings of life. Pueblo is Spanish for village but also refers to their homes modeled after ancient cliff dwellings still seen in the surrounding high desert. They were constructed of adobe, a mixture of clay, straw and ash formed into bricks and dried in the sun. The buildings were roofed with horizontal wooden poles called vigas and these poles extended out past the walls for the characteristic look. Each of the 19 communities had its own distinct character which was displayed best by its pottery. Each pueblo developed different but specific colours and patterns for pottery and these became hallmarks over time. The pueblos remain a vibrant lifestyle today but each varies to the extent of traditions maintained. Some are very traditional while others have assimilated much of modern life. It was a very pleasant and informative visit.

After the tour we returned to the hotel to grab a cab for the 20 minute ride to the Bio Park and were dropped off in the centre's large parking lot. The aquarium and gardens were situated beside each other but the zoo turned out to be some distance away. There was a walkway which we might have undertaken if we had known about it and if we had we could have walked up to the banks of the Rio Grande River and ticked that off my to do list. The normal course for accessing the zoo was either to drive over or take a 20 minute narrow gauge railway ride which departed at quarter past the hour. One entrance fee allowed access to all three attractions plus the train and as we were buying our tickets we found we could catch the next one if we hurried over across a couple of parking lots to the siding. We legged it over.

It was a little cool although sunny with a slight breeze blowing and we weren't in any sense overdressed for the weather. While it was pleasant out of the wind it was almost uncomfortable in the open. We were tough Canadians and used to cool weather so it really wasn't anything hearty souls like us would find to complain about.

The train was a representation of a steam locomotive with a handful of passenger carriages but only a couple of passengers on board. The conductor and engineer traded places every alternate pass and the conductor's main role seemed to be to ensure everybody sat down and stayed sitting down; there was to be no standing on this train. The conductor was quite friendly and after we caught on that we could not stand while the train was moving we chatted the entire ride. The landscape was like most of what we'd seen in Albuquerque - dry, sandy and covered with scrubby trees. Alongside the rails and separated by a chain link fence was the paved walkway that I wished later we had known about as the walk would have been quite nice. Fifty metres or so beyond the pathway was the mighty Rio Grande River. We never got a clear view of that famous waterway but you could tell a river was nearby. It was a shame really that we never saw the Rio Grande because it was referenced everywhere in town. We just never thought about searching it out and so simply missed out on something I would have liked to have seen.

Halfway through the rail journey was a stop at a place called Tingley Beach. This was a series of four manmade lakes (big ponds really) lined in a row alongside the track. Each of the lakes was 100 metres long and about 30 across and was stocked with fish, which drew people out to enjoy a day of fishing. Each lake was stocked with specific-sized fish with its own rules around their capture. Two lakes were catch and release, the third let you keep your catch and the last did not allow fishing at all. This last lake's fish were apparently quite large and were meant for breeding purposes. We could see a major municipal road on the other side of the water and judging by the size of the parking lot it seemed a popular spot.

We have a wonderful zoo at home but climate dictates that certain larger animals would not prosper in a Winnipeg winter. This zoo was a revelation. The complex was sculpted of concrete as you would expect but the pathways between the various exhibits were up and down and roundabout with lots of foliage to help give a sense of the natural environment for the various animals. Even with the cool air I quite enjoyed the walk. The various enclosures all had sculptured curving walls with large windows or open spaces that visitors could look through. It seemed we were seldom at ground level when looking in. I had never before seen white rhinoceroses, ostriches, giraffes, hyenas or wombats, and the only elephants I'd ever seen were at the circus. We passed a large monkey house whose residents appeared just as interested in us as we were in them. There was also touch of home as they had a couple of polar bears and they looked to be the only living things on either side of the walls that seemed to truly enjoy the cool weather.

We wandered about for an hour or so and then found that we were starting to look forward to lunch. The ride back was just as pleasant with the conductor once again chattering all the way, except when telling a Chinese girl three times that she must sit down when the train was moving. Tourists!

By time we got back to the station we were really ready for lunch and we readily outpaced the other passengers in case they were headed for the limited seating restaurant. We soon found ourselves sitting at a table next to a 4 meter by 10 metre long glass wall. It was the aquarium wall, and in deference to those watching us from the other side we declined the catch of the day and opted for hamburgers. Over lunch we finally decided that we were not going to get a rental car and drive to Santa Fe, and so closed that sorry chapter. We felt there was plenty to do around Albuquerque and that we didn't need the aggravation involved in finding where we wanted to go and actually doing the driving. To be honest, we were barely capable of arranging for cabs (as you will soon see). On reflection, the fact we had pre-booked a car may have had something to do with our difficulty in not proceeding. While we had not paid anything for the booking we had arranged it and possibly felt guilty in not following through.

A WOMBAT, I THINK

After lunch we walked through the attraction and watched all sorts of things swimming lazily about. They must have been well fed as nobody seemed in fear of his neighbour. The place housed sharks, big turtles, barracudas, tuna and a host of other large fish that I had no clue as to names. Some were really quite strange looking and it was a fantastic sight. The aquarium was built on one level and had various displays throughout in addition to the main aquarium itself. While we were there a couple of divers were inside the tank cleaning the glass oblivious to the sharks circling above. I mused again that the fish must be well fed. After having lunch alongside the tank the walk through the aquarium was a bit anticlimactic but we enjoyed it just the same.

I have visited a similar large aquarium in Hull, England. That one requires you to go up three floors to the top of the tank. I do mean the top of the tank as you can actually reach over and dip your fingers in the water. The water level was so near the top of the tank that a cup more would cause it to overflow. Once at the top you took a spiral walkway downward round the curved glass to the bottom where you find a glass-walled elevator within the aquarium that returns you to the top. My dad had a fright in that elevator as he turned around just as a manta ray veered off just before touching the glass.

We had yet to see the gardens but neither of us had much urge other than my wanting to see the miniature outdoor railway. It was a nice setup and the fact that it was outside and operated in all weathers was fun. There were a number of rail lines of various gauges with trains chugging around and the various diorama scenes, all of which were well done.

Then it was back to the central courtyard, and luckily so as I needed a bathroom and an ATM. The first provided the necessary relief but the second did not. While I was otherwise engaged Gary had arranged for a cab, a simple task which nearly precipitated an international incident. We had been waiting at the curb a few minutes when a gentleman was dropped off by private car; it became clear he was also awaiting a cab. A yellow cab pulled up and assuming it was ours Gary started to climb in, upon which the other guy raised an objection. Gary insisted it was ours but the cabbie spat out the other guy's name; he then did say he would arrange for another to be sent over. Despite the kind offer Gary contended that we had been screwed over and went on to insist that there was only one cab outfit in town - this based undoubtedly on our vast experience with taxis in Albuquerque. He then wandered mutteringly along back to the office to voice his displeasure and to have them call for another. In passing he was advised that a yellow cab hadn't been called for the first time. As he got back another yellow cab which I suspect was likely sent by the first driver pulled up. As we were clambering aboard a white cab arrived and amid calamitous horn blaring and finger waving gestures we pulled away as yet another yellow cab entered the courtyard. We said nothing to each other.

Our driver was a gregarious older fellow who liked to talk. He regaled us with stories and advice all the way back to the hotel. In another of the never-ending remainders of home he mentioned that his wife had at one time been a sales representative for McCain potatoes, some of which are grown not 50 km from my home. He took us on a different route than the one we had come: down a stretch of the old Highway 66. We saw dozens of motels along the way and although half were closed up all had that 1950s/1960s look. It felt like we were in an old television show or a movie; if it had been night all I would have needed was a slouch hat and a gat to complete the scene.

We were back at the hotel in time for a beer and the making of dinner plans. I found I still had shortness of breath and while I was sure it was the altitude I nevertheless found it a bit disconcerting. Later back at home I watched a program about Denver, which is a mile up just like Albuquerque. The suggestion made by the presenter was that while clearly counterintuitive, at higher elevations a person should work to exhale as much as possible rather than inhale. It seems the issue is getting carbon dioxide out, not getting oxygen in, and has everything to do with the lower density of the air. It seemed plausible to me and it was too bad I hadn't known when I was there so I could have tested it out.

One of the hotel receptionists had previously mentioned that the pueblo museum had a restaurant that served excellent meals. We decided to head there for our supper and had a nice dinner of cornmeal-coated fried chicken. I always enjoy fried chicken but was surprised that Gary with his interest in good healthy food enjoyed it as well. There is one exception to Gary's healthy only policy. He loves pogos, those hot dog things dipped in batter that are then deep fried. To be fair he only succumbs to temptation once a year at the Thunder Bay Blues Festival.

The restaurant was known for its Native American influences and we were quite satisfied by the experience; in fact it was one of the best meals we'd had so far. We each ordered a beer with our meal and as with similar alcoholic-related situations since arriving in Albuquerque we were asked for photo ID. We had been asked to provide same at the liquor store earlier when we had bought our much needed supplies. At the time I thought it had something to do with comparing names on Visa cards. Without any rancour we asked our server, who didn't look old enough to have a drink let alone serve one, why on earth he would ask us for our ID. To require that two retired bankers prove they are the age of majority struck us as slightly ridiculous.

The answer was obvious in its simplicity and at the same time foolish. There is such a problem with drinking and driving in New Mexico that the law of the land was that everyone be asked for ID whenever purchasing liquor. There are such obvious shortfalls to such a system that it would seem the only people this approach would stop are those not old enough. How my being checked for ID when ordering would prevent me from drinking and driving is beyond me. The plot also thickened a bit when we were told that not only was photo ID required every time but vertical cards were unacceptable. This confused us as well. It seems that vertical cards are those with your picture at the top with details beneath. The only acceptable ID is one where the picture is to the right or left of the details. Very strange unless the authorities just wanted to dumb down the process for serving personnel.

Earlier when we had been in the liquor store the guy in front of us had bought a large jug of vodka and two large cans of Red Bull which he told us he intended to use as mix. It seemed that this type behavior would be better served preventing than just a mindless requirement that all patrons have horizontally configured photo identification.

After dinner we spent a bit of time arguing the pros and cons of this approach and reached no reasonable or even rationale purpose to this all-or-nothing process. Surely discretion could be used as it is in most jurisdictions? The discussion was helped along by a couple of brandies. We weren't driving so maybe there was some merit to it after all. After we had explored all the reasons and options we watched the news before calling it a night.

November 17, Thursday

We got moving a little later than normal, and as was now usual Gary went down to the gym to get some exercise and I as was now usual wished him well.

The final and long-pending cancellation of the rental car had triggered a discussion about some other arrangements we had in place. We had pre-booked one night in San Diego at the Dolphin Motel, which was located across the street from the entrance to their fisherman's piers. While the location made sense for access to a waterfront experience we were staying an additional two nights before heading to Portland. We had tentative plans to visit the aircraft carrier Midway and our train left on the last leg from the downtown station at 6:00am. Gary had done some online searching around distances and we had begun to think the Dolphin might not be well situated for the balance of our visit in San Diego and especially for getting to the train station so early in the morning. We now considered a hotel closer to the train station a better idea. Since we were truly enjoying our stay in the Holiday Inn Express we thought we would check about sister hotels in San Diego. Our train west was leaving the next day at 4:45pm and a recent late checkout experience was also front and centre in our minds.

After breakfast we decided to talk to the front desk clerk about it. We were hoping for less of a problem with a late checkout. It turned out there was to be no problem at all because Gary had previously joined Holiday Inn Express's rewards program which entitled him to a 2:00pm checkout. The helpful desk clerk also suggested a couple of Holiday Inn Expresses in San Diego for us to choose from and she offered that the hotel next to Old Town would suit us perfectly. It was newly opened and had a free shuttle to the train station, and since you're already well acquainted with our attitudes towards freebees you can appreciate how such knowledge would impact us. Our clerk also told us she'd lived for a few years in San Diego and provided helpful information about the place. We took her advice and booked the hotel for two nights. I also joined the rewards program as they were offering an immediate 3,000 points which the banker in me could not let escape. It is doubtful I will ever use these points and likely the card will sit unused in my wallet until the next time my kids give me a new one for my birthday.

Those arrangements out of the way we got on with the day. First things always being first we needed a box of beer in case we got thirsty that evening. So we walked across to Walgreens, again. It was an hour before noon and a drunk fellow our age was standing just outside the doors being intently watched by the store's security guard, horizontal photo ID indeed. He was a happy drunk and was awaiting on his female companion who was just inside the threshold of the shop. She and we left via the front door at the same time and we overheard her companion thanking the guard for looking out for his best interests and then wishing him a pleasant day. We returned to our room to park the supplies before we headed out to Nob Hill. This part of town was represented in a number of tourist brochures as a good area to shop. Shopping was not something we did well but to quote an old Paul Newman movie, "sometimes a great notion."

But first I had something of great import to accomplish. The repair on my shoes was continuing apace and to Gary's unending delight. The left shoe had been fixed to my satisfaction but the right was a mystery. I kept the shoe propped toe upright against the wall and seemed to be continually filling the hole with glue. I would squeeze a bit to top it up then I would leave it to dry thinking that should be it. An hour or two later it would be dry but the hole would reappear and require yet more glue. I was unsure if the glue was eating away at the rubber or if the sole was hollow and I was just filling up some huge black hole. In any event I kept at it out of my own diligence and for the added benefit of keeping Gary amused. Once the repair was sorted we again headed down to reception to have them order a cab.

With a forecast of 14C and sunny, I opted for sandals – well, not really opted for as I had no other choice. The reception clerk was very concerned that I was wearing sandals and she was positive I would be cold since it was only going to be 62F in their language. I assured her that we Canadians consider such temperature heavenly and that I would be fine. We told her that Canadians will wear sandals in snow and she was shaking her head violently as we headed out the door.

The cab to Nob Hill at $20 one way turned out to be the most expensive ride of the trip. The area was six or seven square blocks of shops and restaurants on Central with a few more shops up a block parallel to the main drag. With the benefit of hindsight I don't know what we were thinking. Personally I am the "get in and get the hell out" type of shopper and Gary always seems to know exactly what he wants when he walks into a store so the passing or the wasting of time was by definition going to be kept to a minimum. Neither of us was looking to spend anything other than time so it did not bode well for Nob Hill and us. There was lots of noisy traffic headed in both directions but since it was mid week in the middle of November there were few pedestrians about. Nevertheless, there was enough walking traffic to make for a pleasant day. Within an half hour we'd had enough of wandering in and out of shops that while well stocked with all sorts held no interest for us.

So we stopped in at a little coffee shop. The shop was in what had once been a retail store which the owners had tried to transform into a funky place. There was a coffee bar of course but only three or four tables in the huge space. It felt like sitting in a school gymnasium so we chose to sit outside on a patio set and watch the world go by. The place was staffed this day by a couple of young women and we asked the baristas if there was anything around and specifically any bookstores. Gary was still struggling to get into the book he had brought along and was getting quite desperate for something else to read. I appreciated Gary's problems as I have also taken a book away with me that I couldn't quite get into at home. Illogically as it sounds my thinking was that by taking it away with me it would somehow magically transform into a readable book. I am also the type that once I start a book it is next to impossible for me not to finish reading it, no matter how intolerable it is nor how long it takes. I gave my mum a biography of Winston Churchill for Christmas in 1967 that I had commenced to read it many times in the ensuing 40 years. When I retired I resolved to read the thing and forced myself to read a chapter a day until I got through the 1,000 pages. I struggled through it relentlessly and along the way came across a dozen bookmarks from previous failed attempts. It turned out that I actually enjoyed it by time I finished.

The shop staff suggested we looked to be the wrong type of folks to be wandering about Nob Hill, and they offered up that the university was only seven blocks away and that there was of course a bookstore on campus. One of them also said she seemed to recall a small bookstore a block up and parallel to the street we were on. We had earlier been told of this bookstore by a couple of passersby as well but never did find it. As we left the cafe we decided that in addition to not being the sort to find anything in Nob Hill we weren't likely to find much at the university either, so we resolved to wander about a bit more and find a place for lunch. It really was a beautiful day so walking about was a treat and while we retraced a lot of our steps we enjoyed the morning while continuing to ask in vain for directions to the phantom bookstore. Many seemed to agree there was one around but none could exactly recall where it was situated.

Central Avenue was reputed to be part of Route 66 and while I can't confirm that there were a number of old motor hotels and a couple of drug stores on the drag that looked the part. I have no firsthand knowledge of Route 66 other than images from when I was kid. I still see these images today as I relentlessly force Lynn to watch old film noir movies with me.

We stopped for lunch at a restaurant that had once been a Texaco gas station and Ford dealership. The old showroom and front office was the restaurant and the service area was now the food preparation area. The forecourt of the station was set up as an outdoor dining area with dozens of tables and umbrellas. We thought about sitting outdoors but it was just a tad too cold for alfresco dining. I resolved not to mention it to tell the hotel clerk in case she wagged a finger about my sandals along with a chorus of "I told you so." We had pulled pork sandwiches and a beer instead of the usual easy order of a hamburger and once again lunch was terrific though the portions were huge. Why do people complain about huge portions and then proceed to eat up every morsel? We asked our server to order us a cab when we had finished lunch to get us back to the hotel.

Lunch stop on Route 66

Old Route 66 motel, "Nice rooms, free wifi, laundry, pool, colour TV, sushi & sake, what more could you ask?

We were back at the hotel by mid afternoon and found the room had yet to be made up. This finally gave us something to complain about. While the room was being worked on Gary reckoned it was as good a time as any to enjoy a cigar so we went outside to a wind-shielded patio in the warm sunshine. While looking off to the mountains in the near distance I deferred while Gary enjoyed his smoke. Gary only smokes on occasion but when he does he always offers those around him the opportunity to enjoy one of his Cubans. I have partaken of the opportunity over the years but freely admit they are wasted on me and since I don't enjoy them I no longer do, but I have no difficulty with Gary enjoying one. A lazy afternoon seemed to be stretching ahead of us so back in the room we had a beer or two and watched part of the President's Cup from Melbourne, Australia where it was 27C. I can safely say that I had never watched golf on television before and frankly will not do so again. Watching a fly on a window screen is more entertaining.

GARY OUTSIDE THE RESTAURANT AND A CLEAR BLUE SKY

Speaking of a fly on a window screen, just after settling down to a beer and television came the sound of a dog yapping outside. I do like a hotel with windows that you can open. I looked outside and on the boulevard of the service station across the street a gentleman was curbing his West Highland terrier. Gary has always had a Westie for a pet and it seems that no matter wherever I go with him there are always Westies about. On our ramble alongside Hadrian's Wall you couldn't swing a dead cat without hitting one. Anyway, said dog was making all the noise but you couldn't blame the poor thing. On the sidewalk two metres from the little dog was another guy walking his pet on a leash.

The guy on the sidewalk appeared to be about our age. This was bit of a guess really as he had on a hat and I wasn't wearing my glasses but he had that well worn shuffle that folks my age develop after a lifetime of trying to get by. His clothes were a patchwork quite similar to a quilt but well fitted and his pet was wearing a matched set, right down to the hat. This mode of dress may or may not have set the Westie off but the guy's pet would certainly have caused any poor dog consternation. The pet on the leash was a full grown goat – yes, a goat in a coat. Sounds like a Dr. Seuss story. Like other odd situations we'd come across in the past, like a guy on the Hadrian's Wall walk wearing a Supergirl costume, we were both struck speechless. We just stood at the window watching a guy and his well-dressed goat walk off down the sidewalk into the late afternoon sun.

    I was reminded of a line from John Wayne's last movie, *The Shootist*. "I won't be wronged, I won't be insulted, and I won't be laid a hand on. I don't do these things to other people, and I require the same from them." This part of the world is known for its tolerance of individualism and the allowance for anyone to be and do whatever they wish as long as they don't infringe on anybody else. If a man wants to have a goat as a pet and wishes them to have matching suits so be it. But it was getting late and supper plans were pending.

    As must be clear by now I seldom make arrangements for meals when travelling with Gary. There is absolutely no opportunity to miss a meal even if you wish to. I have always found it easier just to wait on him, knowing that about every four hours plans for dining will be underway. Not only does he like to plan early on where to eat, he also needs to know when and within 15 minutes. Just suggesting around such-and-such a time is seldom good enough. That afternoon it turned out I was experiencing some gastric discomfort from lunch's pulled pork sandwich. While hearty it had also been so heavy that I was unsure if I really needed dinner but I hadn't the courage to mention it in case of trouble. Luckily I had somehow talked Gary into stepping out of character and waiting until early evening for dinner.

    Since we'd had such a nice meal at the pueblo centre the night before we walked back there just after 8:00pm. At the previous meal we had noticed a number of stews on the menu that seemed interesting and this night they seemed a good choice for lighter fare. I opted for mutton stew on a chance and was happily rewarded. Strangely we were not carded when we asked for a drink but did not press the point.

On the English walk we had discovered snooker on television and spent a part of each day having a beer and watching an ongoing tournament, each of us choosing a champion and cheering him on over the course of a week. In the evenings after dinner on this trip we discovered a reality show called *Swamp People*. This was undeniably a guilty pleasure and one that neither of us is proud of. The program consisted of a number of families in the Everglades who spent their days hunting alligators. I am unsure what was done with the alligators although apparently some people fancy the meat. The hunters were paid $10 per foot for the beasts, which they captured with some sort of rope noose trap set in trees overhanging their watery homes. Once trapped they were shot and then the carcasses dragged into the hunter's open boat. Sometimes - and it seemed quite often - an alligator was not quite dead when it was time to drag him into the boat. These still-alive creatures always seemed quite reluctant to get into the boat and as you'd expect would fight quite determinedly to avoid it. I didn't understand how at point blank range any of these professional alligator hunters could miss doing away with them but it did make for exciting television.

Like any such business the trade was regulated by a fixed hunting season and the numbers of animals that could be taken was specific. I believe they could take between 100 to 150 animals each in the month long season. The number seemed to be based on how many the hunters took the previous year rather than on conservation. Many of the participants in the show were of a substantial girth (alligator meat must be tasty) and many were missing digits and teeth. Please see above regarding alligators being reluctant to get into boats. After a fine day of chasing alligators the hunters would clean their boats, gear and themselves with pure bleach. This cleaning practice undoubtedly created other problems and issues, if not today then certainly down the road. It was a bizarre show but once you started watching it was hard to turn away. I am happy to say that neither of has watched the program since our return to the kinder gentler climes of Canada; at least neither of us has admitted to it.

This would be our last night in Albuquerque.

November 18, Friday – heading to San Diego via Los Angeles, by way of our old friend The Southwest Chief and The Pacific Surfliner, a day coach.

Just before 8:00am we were eating breakfast with half a dozen other guests on another sunny morning. The common room in addition to the breakfast bar and tables also had a sitting room sectioned off by a couple of sofas facing a gas fireplace above which, in the new insane styling trend, was a large screen television. Is the fireplace the focus of the room or the television? I have recently viewed a television commercial for an internet provider where the actors were watching television in their living room which was above a fireplace. If you can believe it the television had images of a fully stoked fireplace and the real fireplace was cold, madness.

The news that day in the papers and on every channel was the reopening of the case into the death of Natalie Wood. It wasn't really clear if there was any new evidence after all these decades other than the boat's skipper now thinking he knew something that he didn't know then. The papers and especially the television reports were clearly insinuating that Robert Wagner might have had something to do with doing her in. I am writing this some months after the trip and to date they haven't arrested anyone. Sensationalism at its worse. While we were eating and making plans the television further announced that poor old Demi was divorcing a brokenhearted young Ashton. Then and there I resolved that as soon as I got home I would revert back to my usual practice of keeping the damn thing turned off until supper time.

To pass the time before departing for the train station, we decided we would walk about the area near the hotel and then get a takeout lunch from Arby's. Off we went for our walk and there really wasn't much around to see. The area was Indian reserve land and the three or four square blocks around the hotel was just seeing the development of building lots beginning. The landscape was open sandy land with no trees nor any real hint of greenery. A few new buildings had been constructed but they sat forlornly within the neatly laid out roads with for sale signs stuck hither and yon amongst the vacant lots. It looked like it would take some time until the area would be completely developed. As we were wandering down one road off in the distance four guys were espied sauntering along in oversized jackets, hoodies and baseball caps. Instinctively we crossed the road without a word and I was on edge when the "gang" passed by. They were all of 14 years old. I don't know where this instilled fear came from but it was not pleasant.

We checked out at 2:00pm after having fully enjoyed the city of Albuquerque. We grabbed a cab and 25 minutes later were sitting in the waiting room of the station which also housed the bus depot. We had been in a number of cabs over the past few days and while the fares were half what you would pay in Winnipeg or Thunder Bay there was always an additional half a buck cost that was not on the meter. We always paid what was asked as it wasn't really annoying, but it was oblivious and we were leaving town so I asked. It turned out it was a surcharge for having two passengers in the cab and we were told drivers would usually round up to the nearest dollar. It seemed like an odd process.

It had been a pleasant and easy visit. New Mexico is a beautiful state and while it may not have green and lush vegetation the scrub and desert-like environment had a charm of its own. We saw something every day and cabs were reasonably priced and we had received excellent recommendations for meals. Unlike our walk in England, we always took the advice of where to eat when we asked someone for their thoughts and we were never let down. We had no regrets about not driving to Santa Fe. It likely would have been stressful as neither of us enjoys driving if we are not in control of the environment. The only fault I could find was the same we had for Kansas City. There was really very little in the way of pleasant walking around our hotel though that was our own fault. We should have researched better and included areas to walk about into our search for hotels. You can find anything and everything you need on the Internet and if walking about had been a parameter we would have found something to suit. Our primary need for Kansas City had been close proximity to the train station and we wanted to be near Old Town in Albuquerque and we got what we were looking for. If we had done more research we may well have stayed somewhere else but we truly had no regrets.

I continued to have some shortness of breath and while I was not concerned I was annoyed at the aggravation. If only I had seen the reports about spending my energy exhaling rather than inhaling. I imagined if I had stayed a few days longer or got out for a run my body would have gotten used to the thin oxygen. Not to worry, we would be on our way by 4:00pm and since it would be all downhill from here (I just couldn't resist that) the problem would solve itself.

The train station was not much bigger than the one in Depew but was much nicer aesthetically. The wood-constructed building had a cathedral ceiling with adobe tiles on the floor and halfway up the walls. It looked like it had been around for more than 50 years and felt like it too. I sat on the bench people watching for a while. Train travel was much more common here than home and passengers were from all economic classes. At home it tends to appeal to those with plenty of time and money to spend. I am talking about true train travel here not commuter trains which I consider to be nothing more than enormously long buses.

The waiting room was filling up quickly although it was hard to tell if folks had bus or train tickets. The room had a happy vibe to it with people of Indian, Mexican, white, black and other ethnic backgrounds. There was also a common theme, in that everyone but us was dressed in Western clothes. This was cowboy country.

It was not of course all sweetness and light. The restroom was the filthiest place on earth. I was scared to touch anything including the soap dispenser. Hopefully it was a glitch in housekeeping but it was horrible. My mum would have dropped dead in horror or else would have grabbed a mop and along with gallons of boiling water sterilized the place all the while muttering to herself that people are pigs.

There was as yet no sign of The Southwest Chief but I was unconcerned. I knew that at some point shortly friend Gary would get the itch and while trying hard not to would wander up and ask the ticket agent when the train could be expected. He would then return and tell me the train was on time or was expected shortly. This would unquestionably happen a number of times before the train finally did arrive.

In fact he had already been to inquire as he was concerned we could miss our connection at Los Angeles for San Diego if the train was delayed. I on the other hand harboured no such thoughts. I have travelled on enough trains to know there is nowt (a Yorkshire word meaning nothing) you can do about anything. The train will arrive and leave when it does and if we missed our connection I was confident the railway would do everything within its considerable might to make it right. I might have been naïve but truly I was unconcerned and it also helped that we had no firm deadline.

At this juncture I must comment on the seemingly endless array of Gary's foibles that I put on display. They truly were not problems; they were just a part of his makeup and frankly while I make light of them they in no way upset or compromised the enjoyment of travelling with the old fella. I mention this now in the hope that it offsets any of my own slight peculiarities that undoubtedly beleaguered Gary much like the biblical plague of locusts.

ALBUQUERQUE TO SAN DIEGO

Any concerns around schedules were unfounded as The Southwest Chief arrived at 4:35pm and we were promptly on our way 10 minutes later. The train looked to be packed but since we had a compartment our noses were in the air. While on the platform waiting to board a woman mentioned that she too was going to San Diego; like the Lutheran pastor from our previous train ride had mentioned she too was transferring to the south-bound train at Fullerton. We boarded and, as expected and contrary to the porter's directions, Gary went that way down the passage instead of this way. He soon found his way to our compartment though since it is impossible to get lost on a train. There were only two directions one can go after all.

It felt good to be back on board. The ride had become the thing.

I have made a number of comments regarding my travelling companion's lack of comprehension to directions forthcoming from conductors and porters whenever we boarded. Perhaps it was the excitement of a new journey or perhaps the tight circular stairs to the second level turned him around. In all fairness I must confess that I had my own navigational issues and they were sometimes even more comical. I could never seem to remember which side of the carriage our compartment was on and Gary caught me a number of times opening the door to a compartment other than our own. I say a number of times but not all of them for there were a few occasions when he didn't notice that I'd opened a wrong door. I add that generally speaking the occupant of the compartment whose door I opened did notice and happily most were gracious, generally.

As it was close to dinner time Gary was keen to make reservations for the 6:30pm sitting so he went to look for the dining car, which he found closed as we hadn't yet left the platform. Crestfallen he returned but immediately we were underway he went back and found to his gastronomical discomfort that 7:30pm was the earliest seating he could arrange. Karma rewards all good deeds though. Our porter came by just as Gary got back and told us he'd arranged dinner reservations for 5:30pm, if that was okay. I don't have to describe our response and we spent the balance of the time before dinner as we had become accustomed, reading, writing and looking out the window as the world went by.

At dinner I opted for the steak from the same dinner menu we'd seen on our ride from Kansas City. It was not that good I'm afraid, a little on the chewy side. It may not have been the fault of the portion since over the past couple of years I have become less and less fond of steak and now much prefer a chop, chicken or fish. Even at the cottage in the summer I prefer to barbeque pork chops or even hot dogs rather than steak.

Our dinner companion was the woman from the platform who'd told us unbidden that she was going to San Diego via Fullerton as she found the station in Los Angeles too hectic. This alternate route information would prove to be prophetic. The lady was travelling with one of her many teenaged granddaughters to visit one of her many daughters. We were told she always travelled by train and made the trip a couple of times a year. She talked our ears off all through dinner. She clearly had a rich life although not an overly prosperous one and there was a lot of information thrown at us about sickness and marital discord in her and her immediate family's lives; nothing seemed off limits. Occasionally she would pause as if thinking 'should I really have said that to these two Canadian strangers?' Then after a breath she would dive right back into the deep end of the pool offering up information around the salary and staff benefits vis-a-vis part time versus full time employment at Walmart. As with all things if you looked close there was an upside to her constant chatter. She provided details on things to do and see in San Diego and where things were located in relation to the two hotels we would be staying at.

Our new friend would get occasionally annoying over the next half a day as she was always around during meals and she talked relentlessly. Her granddaughter proved to be a treat; the young lady had clearly been in similar situations previously. A couple of times during a nanosecond break in conversation, while her grandmother was taking a much needed breath she would innocently ask, "can I talk now?" But the fact was her grandmother was a really good-hearted woman who'd worked hard all her life without the financial successes that Gary and I perhaps too lightly took for granted. I had a terrific career with the CIBC and I was handsomely rewarded for my toil, even if over the years I occasionally felt underutilized and underpaid. I always attributed those situations to personnel office staff operating beyond their competency levels. Strangely and coincidentally, my two brothers and my sister have all had similar complaints around supervisors in their chosen careers as well.

All joking aside our new friend, and many people we met over the course of our trip, had made their way in life funded by work at retail type places that many of my acquaintances would consider entry level positions. Jobs that young people in our environment would take as a stepping stone to life's work. I have been fortunate and while you could say it was a result of hard work and diligence, was it really? Was part of my success nothing more than an accident of birth? My folks emigrated from England when I was a child and we came to Canada for a better way of life. I have done better economically and educationally than my parents, who in turn did better in the same way than their parents. Will my children's children be so fortunate? Could it have been that our family's relocation and taking part in what a new environment had to offer led to success?

While at dinner we were told that due to our scheduled arrival in Los Angeles at 8:15am breakfast would be served between 5 - 6:00am. I have never been able to eat that early so thought I would likely have to unhappily forgo that prepaid meal other than a cup of tea. But it would turn out not to be an issue.

Later that evening and with some consternation Gary agreed I would get the lower berth on this leg of the journey. I'd taken the upper on the Chicago to Albuquerque run so technically and democratically it was my turn. We agreed to flip for the lower berth for the Los Angeles to Portland leg. While I would find the upper berth more comfortable I did fancy a window next to me whilst in bed. There would have been no issue if there had been an upper window as I would have willing slept up for the entire tour but as there wasn't we had to deal with this minor irritation. I don't think Gary particularly cared if there was an upper window or not; I think he just didn't want to sleep in the upper berth.

At just about 7:30pm we crossed the Continental Divide. We actually were only aware of this from the information provided in the train brochures as it was too dark to see out the window. The Divide is the point where all running water flows towards the Pacific, rather than east to the Atlantic or north through to Hudson Bay in my home province of Manitoba. But something else was going on that took away from that monumental highlight. Since leaving Albuquerque there had been a couple of minor commotions and we were of the opinion that there may have been a crazy person on board. We had noted a skinny, scruffy long-haired fellow on the platform in Albuquerque (his appearance not to be confused with my own well-developed, decades-long scruffy style kind of look). We didn't share our thoughts at the time but it later transpired that each of us had decided that the guy might prove troublesome. Since dinner he had passed through our car a number of times muttering loudly to himself with the occasional cuss thrown in to liven up the language. The latest diatribe was directed the porter's way and had something to do with either the quality of the service or the fare offered in the dining car. Our only female porter of the trip was a confident looking young woman who appeared tough enough to handle anything that came her way. With the patience of Job she tried for some time to help the passenger but now suggested that she'd call the conductor down to the carriage but this didn't lessen the tirade.

Readers appreciate by now that sleeping cars use all space economically and that passageways between both sides of the carriage are really just one person wide. You can imagine someone with issues that they wish to impart verbally to staff is nigh on impossible to do so privately, and that is assuming the person doing the conversing wishes the tale to be private. This fellow had no such urge. It was unavoidable to overhear and uncomfortable for all within ear shot. Within a few moments was an announcement over the intercom calling the conductor to the dining car and we assumed it was related to our upset fellow passenger.

Things seemed to settle down and around 9:30pm we were stopped at Winslow, Arizona and I was humming *Take It Easy* by the Eagles. The station looked to be 100 years old and right out of a Zane Grey story. The paint on the wooden casement windows was peeling and the platform was covered with a gabled wooden roof. It seemed like a good time for a drink so we went forward two carriages to the club car, then down to its lower level to get a beer. The bar had just opened and it was quite a wait since in addition to serving drinks it also offered up microwaved hamburgers and the like. Not everyone on board had meals included with their ticket and this was a noticeably thriftier option than the dining car. About a dozen people stood waiting in front of us but as we were on 'train time' we weren't put out in the slightest. At least not at first.

The lower level of the club car was accessed by a stairway from the second level in the middle of the carriage. The bar was at one end with the balance of the space allotted to four or five yellow Formica topped booths like the ones you see in old diners. Some people utilized these booths to enjoy their libations and some were using them to wait on friends standing in line. The booth directly opposite the bottom of the stairway and right beside where Gary and I were waiting in line was occupied by a couple of middle-aged guys. The younger of the two was cleanly shorn and shaved, stood six foot tall, likely weighed 250 lb. and appeared in awe of his companion. That guy was about four inches shorter, 100 lb. lighter and was bearded with a braided pony tail half way down his back. He was wearing a jean jacket with the arms roughly cut off to better which show off his tattoos. To suggest that these fellows were rough looking would be an insult to "rough looking" and I was quite immediately uncomfortable. Moments later a senior citizen about five foot five shouted at them "what type of beer do you want?" from the bar some 15 feet away. I missed the response but it apparently did not really make a difference to them. The senior citizen came by us and sat down at the table and it would be no understatement to say he was missing the majority of the teeth God had given him. It turned out the old-timer was the father of one of the guys in the booth, although of which one was never made quite clear and I was too polite to ask.

My discomfort level did not recede with this new addition to the booth. The three of them spend what seemed like hours discussing the pros and cons of the various state correctional facilities they'd had the misfortune of enjoying in the tri-state area. If you're taking notes, apparently Folsom should be given a miss if at all possible, San Quentin isn't that bad, but if you really must go to prison New Mexico is the best place in which to enjoy state hospitality. One of them - I didn't have the nerve to turn around and see who was talking - did mention that he couldn't afford to go back to jail in California as he would be subject to the 'three strikes and you're out' law. Weird, scary and sad all at the same time. I noticed that this last exchange was overheard by the gentlemen in line in front of me. He clearly was hanging on to his 12 year old daughter with a much firmer hand than when we first got in line.

You can meet people from both ends of the evolutionary scale on a train.

We finally got our beer and couldn't wait to go upstairs. We felt we would more fully enjoy our beverages in the comfortable surroundings of the upper level rather than the Formica booths. This clearly was the climax of our evening so after we finished off our beers we headed back to the compartment. The berths had been made up and I read *Robinson Crusoe* (who set sail from my birth home, the port of Hull) for a little while and watched the world pass by my window in the moonlight. Before drifting off to sleep I wondered if the three ex cons in the bar would be up all night. For some reason I have always imagined that ex cons need less sleep than I.

November 19, Saturday

Next thing I knew it was 7:15am and we were coming into Barstow, California. We had slept through most of Arizona and our train was over two hours behind schedule. While we slept like the dead a freight train had broke down on the main line. This resulted in our sitting on a siding somewhere between Flagstaff, Arizona and Needles, California (famous as the home of Snoopy's brother). The stop had clearly not interfered with our rest as we were blissfully unaware of the lay by. We would not be arriving in Los Angeles anywhere near on time but that was of no concern to us. Our train to San Diego was a commuter and it made the run every three-quarters of an hour.

Along with the changes to the schedule the view out the window had also changed dramatically. We had been descending towards the coast for some time and the mountains while still visible were now some distance away. It was hilly though with lots of sagebrush around and the landscape was once again the dusty browns we had seen in New Mexico. We were also clearly back in civilization. Numerous tracks were now running alongside and many trains passed by in both directions and incredibly close. If the window were open you could have touched one as it passed by although at the speed they were travelling it would have had your arm taken off.

Our previous night's dining companions joined us for breakfast. The older one continued to talk almost nonstop even while chewing and provided ample information that we were sure would prove helpful in navigating San Diego. Today I had a better chance to enhance my opinion of this good-natured soul who I'd decided was likely in her 60s. We learned that after spending a life time at menial work in restaurants and retail stores she was now babysitting children in retirement to provide a crust. Once again I marveled at how lucky my life had been. Here we were travelling by train by choice and she and her granddaughter and many others were travelling by rail for solely economic reasons.

The urban scenery outside was now similar to the very beginning of our journey. We were travelling alongside very depressed areas of human habitation and it was not pretty. It was a view we would never have seen by any other mode of transport and it was unexpected. An unexpected happier view came upon us when, travelling through a massive rail marshalling yard, we noticed a couple of Canadian National Railway box cars and we both immediately thought of home. There were more and more railway lines out the window now and an enormous train with four locomotives passed us going the other way loaded just with semi-trailers. Unloading of the cargo must be a case of hooking up a truck and then quite efficiently just driving away. Freeways were now also coming into view and they were like something from a Jetson's cartoon: wide, high and coming and going in every direction with those large green highway signs spanning the byways wherever you looked.

The weather was definitely not what I expected of California either. The clouds were heavy and close but with the occasional sunny spot. The low clouds blocked the view of the tops of the hills, they weren't mountains anymore. Rain was likely in the forecast as we came into San Bernardino and here we got sight of our first palm trees. Many of the towns and cities we were passing through had recognizable names which helped to offset the sadder views and the weather.

It was just before 8:00am when we saw the first bit of green grass we'd seen for quite some time. I'm inclined to say since Kansas City though that couldn't possibly be right. We were not in Kansas anymore and I was unsure if I liked it.

This country seemed to have an enormous number of vehicle wrecking yards and uncountable numbers of private homes with non-running vehicles pushed to the back of properties alongside the rail line. Gary and I spent some time discussing the opportunity of developing some sort of mobile auto crusher/compacter that we could use to travel America cleaning up these old wrecks. We reckoned the market opportunity alongside the rails alone would be sufficient to provide profitable work for years to come. One could likely even use the railway to transport the crushed and compacted product to recycling operations. The planning and discussions around this obvious golden money making opportunity ended as quickly as they arose.

Along with cars, yards were filled with abandoned motorcycles, trailers, buses, and trucks and scores of Cadillacs. You could well say an overabundance of them. I guess even poorer folk need status cars but I'd have been willing to bet that most of the Cadillacs we were looking at had been well worn when acquired by the last owner. There is a truly a car culture in this part of the country. In addition to the scrap vehicles most of the driveways seen from the train window always seemed to have two vehicles. I shouldn't be too critical about the car culture in the U.S. I spend my life trying to maintain three vehicles, two motorcycles and a couple of boats. In the bigger picture our local economy is built on the sale of vehicles and this is readily proved by newspaper advertising. Our daily paper has a car dealer's ad on every other page plus a two section supplement around cars in every Friday edition.

When you get down to thinking about cars it is clear that they are what drive just about everything in our economy and our lives. Big box stores wouldn't exist without a way to get there. Would McDonald's and sundry restaurants be all over the place if we had to walk or take the bus to enjoy (?) their fare? Would a convenience store be on every street corner flogging smokes, pop and chips if we weren't able to drive by? It would seem that rather than being a convenience to help us the car has turned us into a society that stops and shops as the whim strikes. We no longer plan and execute as our grandparents or even our parents did.

I recently read that the first packaged foods were only developed in the 1930s and since that time an adult's average weight in developed countries has increased by over 12 kilos. In the same period the personal ownership of cars has skyrocketed from being a luxury item to a life requirement. Is there a relationship?

Later while lazing about the club car we overheard talk that they had put someone off the train overnight. We immediately assumed it was our guy from Albuquerque who'd made such a bother of himself throughout the preceding day. It was not hard to imagine that someone who found something wrong with everything would go over the edge while the train was stopped waiting on a siding for two hours in the middle of the night. It seemed odd that somebody who had the benefit of a sleeper which included meals could not be just be as comfortable as we were. Why couldn't he just sit back and enjoy the ride? We later heard that the malcontent was shown the door in Needles. I guess conductors have grown more civilized over the years as they ensured the train was stopped before the passenger was flung off. We never were sure that it was in fact him but we never did see our suspected victim again.

We were well and truly behind schedule and were not going to make our purchased connection in Los Angeles. Happily in addition to information we received from a couple of passengers, notably the constant talker, it had now even been recommended by the conductor that we get off in Fullerton and grab the first Pacific Surfliner bound for sunny San Diego. The train we were booked on to leave Los Angeles would be on its way before we arrived, but in a remarkable situation that train would be coming back through Fullerton on its way to San Diego. We had a good chance of catching it and could well end up arriving in San Diego on time. Almost like getting there before you leave.

A week tomorrow we would be on our way home. We still had a lot of ground to cover and things to see or as some wag once said, "I've got rats to catch and cats to kill" - or was it the other way round?

We arrived in Fullerton just after 9:00am and wandered out of what looked like a brand new station directly onto the westbound platform. We then went up and over a walkway to the southbound platform to await our connection. We had just missed a train by minutes and it was in fact the one that we had been booked on. It would have been nice to have made it just for the pleasure of saying we were late but ended up arriving on time.

It was only to be a short wait and it was a beautiful sunny morning as we rested on one of dozens of outdoor benches set amongst large palm trees providing cover from the sun. It was quite pleasant to sit and breathe fresh air after a day on the train. There were about 30 people waiting with us and I would say most were from the same economic strata as us. Everyone on the platform was white and most would soon be seeing 60 if they hadn't already stared it down. It was odd to be in a group of people of that size and there not be any Native-Americans, Latinos, Afro-Americans, or any of the other visible minorities for that matter who had been part of our lives over the past week. There didn't appear to be any undesirable element alongside Track 5 in Fullerton this day. It would seem the lower economic strata passengers on board were headed to Los Angeles which by happy happenstance included our penal system experts from the previous evening.

Sitting quietly as Gary wandered off to find a drink of water I recognized the smell of the air. It reminded me of Mexico with its damp and fragrant, heavy sweet smell. I also realized and not for the first time that I had lost track of time again, not the hour but the day. I was also hard pressed to figure out how long we had actually been on the train.

Our chatty friend and her granddaughter soon found me and continued on with the never-ending story of her life that I had by now become enamoured with. When Gary returned she continued to fill us in on family history and over the course of the discourse we discovered that while she looked 10 years older she was in fact our age. I say discourse but it really wasn't as she talked and we nodded. She'd had a tough life but it didn't seem to have impacted her enjoyment of it at all.

Someone had discarded a pile of nuts on the pavement just to our left and a half dozen gulls swooped in to clean them up in a matter of seconds. The gulls reminded me of a day in Thunder Bay in the mid 1980s during a period when the bank had decided to post me there. The family had gone down to a lakeshore park for the day and the kids who were 6 and 4 were enjoying running about munching popcorn. All the while a flight of gulls were circling and following them. From time to time the girls would throw popcorn out for them. As we got back to the car one alighted on the roof. I am not sure alighted is the right word as the thing was as big as a cocker spaniel. It then refused to move despite numerous and loud shoos from us. We soon bored of this and considered that if we got into the car and slammed the doors the bird would get the message. Well, we were wrong and even the starting of the car didn't shift the squatter. We ended up driving away unsure as to when he flew off. If this seems cavalier to the bird's well being I mention that I have always considered gulls nothing more than flying rats.

By 10:15am and sensing warm weather we were comfortably ensconced in the very full day coach of The Pacific Surfliner on our way to San Diego which lies just twenty miles from Mexico.

Our trip from Chicago on The Southwest Chief had been heartily enjoyed. There had been four or five different crews and three different trains but the service was seamless. It was quite a change for us to now sit with the rabble after the luxury of a compartment but since it was only a short trip we would cope. The Pacific Surfliner was more like a bus and it didn't have the feel of a train somehow. But some things don't change and once again Gary needed directions immediately after receiving them. This time the confusion was around a group of four facing chairs that he wanted to sit at but which I had said were unavailable. I wasn't overly clever - a clearly posted sign said the spaces were reserved for families. He wondered out loud how come I always seemed to know what was what when it came to moving about the train. I simply pointed out that while he was wandering off to figure out what was what my approach was to simply look around and listen to instructions as they were given or posted.

An hour into our journey it seemed like we had stopped at a station every 10 minutes and it was getting annoying. Then we turned left at the Pacific Ocean and everything changed. Our car was now only half full and we were barreling right along. Out the window the water stretched away as far as you could see. The ocean was a dull grey, not the beautiful turquoise green of the Caribbean but still spectacular. In places we seemed to be only metres from the water's edge; then there would be a clump of civilization with a number of houses between us and the sea. When it was just the beach between us and the Pacific it was quite the idyllic view what with dolphins leaping, fishermen casting from the beach, boats chugging out and folks surfing or sun bathing. There were also occasional bunches of small cabanas that I guessed were rental accommodations every couple of miles. It was beautiful and everything a prairie boy like me expects when he thinks of Southern California (though nobody was actually swimming).

Half an hour later we had moved away from the shore. People had populated the area along the coast for obvious reasons and the rail line had to move inland along a little raise in elevation but with still spectacular views. The urban landscape was hugely different than what we had seen out the window recently. The people along this rail line lived at a substantially higher level. The homes and property out the window were almost unimaginably expensive.

OUR FIRST LOOK OF THE PACIFIC OCEAN

We arrived in San Diego with someone looking out for us. There were two train stations in San Diego, one in Old Town and one downtown. Left to our own devices we would have undoubtedly disembarked at the Old Town Station. However, somewhere along the trip we overheard someone suggest there were no cabs to be had at Old Town so we rode on through to the terminus of the line. But life is such that good luck can always be expected to be offset by the other and it was here we had our first real bit of aggravation.

Judging by the line ups of cars outside the station there appeared to be a dozen cab companies in town and each had populated their driving staff with new arrivals of eastern European or African descent who to a man had difficulty with the Queen's English. On top of that we were soon to learn there wasn't a cab driver in the city who seemed to know where anything was. To counter these minor shortcomings they all relied completely on handheld computer GPS's to find locations. They would only consult the device once underway and only when the cab had achieved warp speed. Then, in an effort to prove how proficiently they could drive, the need to observe posted speed limits was gratuitously ignored. Combine such aplomb with the obviously expected lack of English language-spelling ability while inputting addresses into a GPS and you can only imagine the ride, well actually you can't. All our rides here were to prove hair-raising and very similar to Space Mountain.

A dozen years ago I had taken my children to Disneyland for a holiday and they had insisted on going to Space Mountain first. The entire ride was undertaken with eyes closed tight. Unlike that ride San Diego cab rides were undertaken with eyes forced wide open. But there were similarities since in both situations I found myself praying for a quick and painless death. On at least three occasions during our short time in San Diego we had to suggest in pleading tones to a cab driver that the light had truly changed red some time ago and perhaps watching the road rather than the GPS might be inherently safer than the approach he was undertaking.

I have gotten ahead of myself. We actually had climbed in and out of two different cabs at the train terminus, a classy way of saying the end of the line. It was unbelievable. You get in a cab and then have to get out and find another because the driver doesn't know or understand where you are going even though he has the assistance of a guy on the sidewalk who may or not be a supervisor. It was possible he was just an interested citizen who came round to the driver's window to chat about our destination choice but we never knew. We would have leapt from the second cab as well but we were immediately trapped and underway.

The first block of the journey had the driver leaning back over the front seat to inform us a couple of times that the address quoted was not in San Diego. Where we came from drivers generally face the direction the vehicle is moving. Notwithstanding our obvious ignorance around where we were going he did ultimately find the Dolphin's address on his GPS. We were deposited on the forecourt in a quarter of an hour. It turned out to be a $20 cab ride (or amusement ride, depending on perspective).

Gary had found this Route 66-era motel on the Internet and we were booked into Room 30 at $70 a night. I was still on edge from the cab ride and since I already had some concerns about the Dolphin when the owner innocently asked if we were staying three nights I spat out, "no, one night." I think Gary was taken aback by my outburst but we had decided in Albuquerque that we would only stay the one prepaid night and then move on to the Holiday Inn Express. I had just wanted to make sure there were no misunderstandings. We were told the room was still being tidied but that it was okay to go up. When we got to the room a chatty Oriental woman went out of her way to tell us it was a wonderful place to stay as she was finalizing the finishing touches.

The Dolphin was a two-storey motel across the street from the entrance to San Diego's fisherman's pier and docks. It had an outdoor stairway to the second floor rooms that were accessed from an outdoor walkway. The building was aligned in a stubby "L" with our room just past the joint of the two arms. The place had a *CSI* crime scene sort of look to it. There was no view out of the front and the small back window overlooked the neighbouring business's parking lot. The room itself was only about three meters square with a double and a single bed. I snagged the double with no complaint from Gary, not that I gave him a chance to complain. A small refrigerator doubled as an end table and a smallish television was stuck up high on the wall as there really was no other place for it. It was plugged into a white extension cord that hung down the wall to the socket. This was something that would have driven my *House Beautiful* partner Lynn's sensibilities off the deep end.

There was also a small open closet that was not big enough for both our bags. In fact a cat would have been unable to turn around without stepping out. The place had a functional if not tight bathroom which retained its original tile shower stall and in which said cat would have had the same issue. The entire place was painted white, bright white, both walls and ceiling and very thick while paint at that. The place was very, very clean but small and featureless with the exception of the window air conditioner. It was a window type unit but had been installed permanently in the wall and likely installed where it was because it was so big it would have taken up the entire window. The thing was huge. Its front was as big as the top of the desk I am writing this on. In addition to being big the noise it made when turned on was incredible. Happily it was not hot enough to warrant using the behemoth.

The place catered to fisherman who took advantage of the nearby fishing wharf. Many establishments have a sign banning guests in the rooms after certain hours but this place had a notice banning fish in the rooms. The price was a third cheaper than the Holiday Inn but the difference in little luxuries, like having to go outside to exhale, were just a little too draconian for me. We both sheepishly agreed to call the place adequate. I mean there wasn't even a telephone in the room, likely a good thing as there was really no space for one. There was an upside to the stay and that was a free breakfast. This was served on the outdoor forecourt and under umbrellas in case of rain.

The overpowering whiteness of the place reminded me of a coworker Max that I had the pleasure of working with for a number of years. In a particularly dreary period of our employment he and I discussed alternate opportunities for earning a living and kicked around various businesses that might be attractive to guys of our abilities and sensibilities. Something easy to manage and without the many and various headaches that banking customers routinely threw at you every 12 minutes of every day. I suggested a paint store but not a traditional paint store. We would only stock one colour and that being white and only one shade of white at that. After talking about it in depth it seemed like a wise approach. Our overheads would be quite low since we could utilize many suppliers and we wouldn't really need much of a label, if in fact we even needed labels. Customers could even bring their own buckets if they wished. Staff training costs would be minimal and returns would be nonexistent. Marketing and advertising would be simple as everything would be white - fixtures, shelving, furniture, staff uniforms, delivery vehicles, everything on the premises would be white. Yes everything would be white. You want to talk about "branding" - we would be known far and wide as the white paint guys and surely people would quickly get it.

We even came up with a motto- "You want white paint - we got white paint - You want some other colour - get the hell out".

Then we hit the snag. If everything was white and if that was our raison d'être how could we put up signs, how would we advertize, how would we ring up sales? We both felt that compromising the strategic strength would doom the project immediately. We were snookered and so put the thing on the back burner until such time as we could sort it out. It's not dead yet as yet and we still discuss it whenever we meet, but I have to be honest that I am not hopeful.

THE DOLPHIN

To be very fair to the Dolphin it was a nice clean tidy place, just not as nice as I was looking forward to.

Once settled we needed something to eat and since it was way past traditional lunch time we quickly headed across to a restaurant recommended by the hotel staff. The place was on the water and was packed with people. We stepped up to the counter and ordered a meal which in our case included a beer from the help yourself cooler. Within minutes our order was shouted out. We went outside to the patio and enjoyed our repast looking out over moored fishing boats and across the bay to the San Diego downtown. The sun was shining and it was warm and we were very comfortable.

SIGN ON THE COURTYARD WALL OF THE DOLPHIN

I had decided on a sandwich of two huge breaded crab cakes stuffed between two slices of white bread with chips and a beer. No one really needs a crab cake sandwich. I could have ordered a crab meat sandwich but no. I was stuffed like a Christmas goose and it was all I could do to move for a while. When I could finally comfortably stand we headed out for a walk along the boardwalk that started just outside the restaurant and ran alongside the shoreline.

There was all sorts of development along the water including restaurants, warehouses, business and ship offices. Along the length of the walkway docks ran out into the water, alternating between pleasure craft and working boats. We wandered along for about three quarters of an hour towards downtown when the walkway suddenly stopped at an old warehouse. On the way back we moved inland a block and walked along a main road that was packed with restaurants and hotels. As we were always on the lookout for our next meal we noticed a pizza place that we thought would be a good choice.

San Diego Marina, pleasure craft

Without a care in the world we walked further along from our motel enjoying the fresh air. Clearly this was a prosperous city and we were impressed with its cleanliness and seemingly friendly people. Granted, we only could speak to the area we were in but what we saw was great. When we got back to the Dolphin we put our feet up and read the papers and watched the news and it was quickly clear the room was not really conducive to spending a lot of down time in.

Dinner was a little later than usual because of our late lunch. The pizza joint we'd seen earlier proved to be a very popular place and was packed solid with an hour waiting time when we walked up. We deemed it not worth our time so buggered off, which was a mistake. We ended up in a fish shop down by the water close to where we'd had lunch. I had rock cod and chips and Gary crab cakes. It was nice fare but there were only a few of us in the place and the ambience was less than stellar. Plus I was still stuffed from lunch. It was here that I had the worst cup of coffee I've ever had and that is saying something. It would have stripped paint off a battleship's hull and I would have complained voraciously if the waitress hadn't specifically told me she was going to make a fresh pot especially for me, if I wouldn't mind waiting. I shudder to think what the leftover from the previous pot would have been like.

SAN DIEGO, WORKING CRAFT

After the meal we again walked about the shore and passed a guy fishing from the walkway. I would have bet there were no fish about since dozens of craft were coming, going or moored and the water wasn't the cleanest. Amazingly that was not the case and the fisherman said he regularly caught halibut and barracuda from the very spot. You would think that a fish could find a much more hospitable locale. He offered up that he had once caught a metre-long halibut and had very recently caught one just under that size. He said it in such away as if apologizing for his lack of talent. I gushed that a metre is a pretty big fish where we came from, at which he reconsidered and said "yeah, you're right it is a big fish."

When we returned to the Dolphin we turned the television on and had a couple of brandies before calling it a night. We hadn't seemed to get much accomplished but this was similar to our experience in Kansas City and Albuquerque. We seemed to be slow moving when just off the train.

We were to head off to the Holiday Inn Express Old Town in the morning, but not until after our free breakfast of course.

November 20, Sunday

Up at 8:40am - the room turned out decent enough that I'd slept well. This was odd considering that the neighbours were talking loudly over their television well into the morning hours and that it poured down rain for quite a while. There also had been a lot of sirens off in the distance and a car alarm had gone off at 6:00am which would have normally tried my patience. Yet I still say I had a good night's sleep, go figure.

We had awakened at seven, and since two people couldn't stand in the room at the same time Gary went down to get a couple of coffees, muffins and a paper. It was still raining a bit so dining alfresco seemed like an odd idea. When the rain tapered off I went for a walk while Gary got ready for the day. The previous evening I had noticed a newer BMW motorcycle parked alongside the office and now as I was admiring it the owners walked up. They looked to be in their late 40s and they volunteered they were from France and were on their way around the world. They were a bit tentative at first until I mentioned I was Canadian whereupon they immediately broke into a long tale of how they had just returned from Montreal and the Canadian east coast where they had particularly loved the Gaspe Peninsula. It is one thing to tour by motorcycle on your own but two up on a round-the-world trip would really test comfort and compatibility factors.

My new friends told me that they were on their way to Patagonia and the tip of South America the next morning but first they were heading to a BMW dealership to have the bike given a once over. I got the sense that BMW was providing some measure of support on their adventure. When I mentioned I had once owned a similar model they really wanted to chat. It is the same everywhere, if you mention you're a motorcyclist to another you're instant friends. We parted with me wishing them well and to take particular care while in Mexico. The news from that country had not been pleasant for some time, what with drug runners, kidnappings and murders seemingly occurring hourly.

I do admit to having thoughts of undertaking a long motorcycle trip of my own. I have often kicked it about but have yet to pull the pin.

Later over another coffee Gary and I decided on a last walk around the neighborhood before checking out. We both were a little uncomfortable about leaving after only one night since we had initially inquired about staying for three. When we booked they had only required one prepaid night so that's all we did. We felt wrong somehow and didn't even want them to know that we were changing hotels. It was a nice clean reasonable place but it was a just little too short on amenities for our liking, especially mine. So let's be honest we were feeling guilty.

The morning walk was along the same boardwalk we'd sauntered along previously. Last evening we had come across an old-timer seemingly in good although deranged spirits who had been singing a KISS song to himself. This morning he was clutching a sleeping bag and swearing while twisting about this way and that. He clearly had spent the night outdoors and just as clearly had some real mental health issues. Why was he out on his own and how did he manage? He seemed in no danger so we guiltily left him and continued down a road heading away from downtown.

It would be professional to provide more comprehensive directions but we had no idea on which point of the compass we were headed. Two blocks down the road we came across another marina and by the look of the forest of masts these were mostly sailboats. Just off in the distance were a number of high rise apartment buildings overlooking the bay; unquestionably they were not rent-subsidized places.

About an hour later we were back at the Dolphin and in the interests of a quick and clean getaway we grabbed our bags, checked out and asked the desk clerk to order a cab without mentioning where we wanted to go.

The cab to the Holiday Inn Express – Old Town cost $15 and was the most hair-raising ride of them all. As mentioned cab drivers seemed to totally rely on their GPS and this guy was no exception. He would have driven us right through a red light if Gary had not expressed alarm, and with some conviction, that the light was good and truly red. Clearly unperturbed by almost killing his fares and any subsequent impact on a forthcoming tip he proceeded to drive right through the next stop sign. To be kind I might suggest he coasted through but the effect on us was the same. The cab rides might have been cheaper than home but that did not adequately offset the danger undertaken when travelling in one. We arrived at the hotel in one piece to find the front desk clerk less than civil when we walked up. Remarkably her demeanor changed completely when we said we had a reservation. She then couldn't have been more helpful. Perhaps she'd been initially put on edge by the look of two disheveled travelers with eyes still bugged out from a death-defying cab ride that she knew nothing about.

Without any question this hotel was a better choice for us. It was a much bigger room in a newly renovated hotel complex with all expected amenities. The Dolphin had been okay to sleep in but not so great to spend time in. And we were now also closer by half to downtown. The place was up on a hill and our room overlooked the distant bay with a five-lane freeway and the airport between it and us. The noise from the roadway was not overpowering when the window was open but traffic was incessant. We decided to reconnoiter for an hour or two, and discovered that while the hotel claimed to be in Old Town adjacent to might have been more accurate as it was good walk away.

Just after 2:00pm we took a $12 ride down to the harbour. With all our complaints about cabs you would expect we would have been reluctant to use them, but we had little choice.

Gary and I always seem to have a great deal of luck on trips and this day was no exception. Our goal was to see and tour the USS Midway aircraft carrier, and when we arrived at the waterfront we discovered that San Diego was hosting an America's Cup yachting event. Our planned destination was at the junction of a road running along the waterfront and one intersecting it from downtown. Thousands of people were about and just as many cars and all under the control of traffic police. Seamlessly they allowed throngs of pedestrians and cars to take their turns.

Why did the chickens cross the road? To see the America's Cup.

The waterfront was filled with people and the water was filled with racing yachts and we had to wander through the excitement of the staging area to reach our destination. Unfortunately, we could not snag an invitation to take part in the festivities. The hospitality Moet Champagne bar with its fancy canapés looked particularly enticing. While free for participants the ticket fees for event passes were well beyond our meager resources. That being said, we were allowed to walk about to view the beautiful yachts and gawk at the beautiful people - and gawk we did. The boats were magnificent and we were close enough to a couple to see how they were put together, the boats that is, not the beautiful people.

A large crane with canvas slings would pick incredibly the expensive craft off the wharf and place them in the water. Then they were moved about by zodiac-type boats acting as tugs. We stood about and watched as a couple headed out into the harbour. They were beautiful and graceful and made no noise with the exception of the occasional clang of a bell, the creak of a mast or the flap of a sail in the slight breeze.

AMERICA'S CUP YACHTS, USS MIDWAY TO THE LEFT

After half an hour of looking at the people and the yachts we made our way through a couple of passageways and down past a number of old warehouses to arrive on a jetty where the Midway was berthed. We had no inkling how close the ship was because our view had been obstructed by the tight roadway running between buildings. When we did get onto the jetty our first view was incredible. At first glance the ship looked like a two block long ten storey steel grey building. I have a fair understanding of Archimedes' principle, but how does something so big float? I wonder alike how a 747 can actually fly.

The brochure informed us that the USS Midway was commissioned in 1945 and was the largest ship in the world for 10 years. It was the first ship too large to pass through the Panama Canal. Its construction cost was $90 million with a further $260 million spent on a four-year overhaul in 1966. Consider these other facts about her:

- Her engines generated 212,000 horsepower and she weighed 69,000 tons.
- Two thousand feet of anchor chain were attached to 20-ton anchors that were 335 metres long and 79 metres wide.
- She was driven by propellers six meters high, had 18 decks from bottom to top and her flight deck covered four full acres.
- Her fuel tanks held nearly 3.5 million gallons and when underway went through 100,000 gallons of fuel a day (260 gallons per mile). The crew of 4,500 also used a lot of fuel - 10 tons of food a day.

This was a big ship.

The Midway cruised all the world's seas and served in most American wars until decommissioning in 1992. In 2004 she became a static display known as the USS Midway Museum in San Diego and by 2011 five million people had visited.

After paying admission on the jetty you entered the ship by going up a two-storey double-wide stairway built on the dock. At the top of the stairs you passed through a door in the hull remarkably smaller than you'd expect. The ticket taker made a point to tell all and sundry to 'mind your head as you go.' The area you entered was as wide as a football field and stretched the full length of the ship directly beneath the flight deck. The area could be described as similar to a giant gymnasium with seemingly no interior walls.

I have had an unexplainable and long time distrust of the militarization, security measures and comfort with firearms that is on display in the U.S. and so have always been ill at ease when visiting there. As a result I have only visited four times in 40 years. I don't have a problem crossing into Europe, Latin America or the Caribbean - just into the United States, the so-called land of the free. I am just on edge when there and I know it's all in my head. I relate this because as we entered the ship we were funneled single file through a queue and everyone had their picture taken and without permission asked for first. If you wanted the picture they would sell you one but I had the paranoid sense that the selling of photos was not the primary function around the taking of pictures. I'll now repeat that there had been five million visitors in six years; paranoid, I think not. I am certain there was some nefarious reason for the picture taking and this did not improve my impressions of the military type nature of America.

The first deck we entered was crowded with displays, one a model of this ship and a new one under construction that would be even larger than the Midway. There were also a dozen or so single-seater airplanes of various vintages, a simulator display of space and jet modules and, of course, a shop selling very well-priced souvenirs. The hundreds of people milling about were efficiently marshaled by retired veterans wearing leather aviator jackets and mirrored sunglasses.

We were offered rides on the simulators but I saw little need or desire to pay for the opportunity to throw up my breakfast so declined the opportunity, as did Gary. Continuing along we just followed the crowd and found ourselves down a deck in the crews' living areas. It was as antiseptic as you would imagine of something made of steel with everything painted grey (perhaps Max and I could make a go of a grey paint store). I was forever ducking my head and I wondered why all the doorways and ceilings with their exposed pipes and conduits were so low. I am five foot eleven and a bit and can only imagine that many of the crew over the years would have been my size. Likely there were a lot of concussions recorded over the 40-plus years this ship was in service. It seemed unlikely that the designers of such an enormous thing would have overlooked the height of those who would be expected to serve on board so perhaps there was an engineering reason to 'mind your head'.

Everything on board seemed familiar. I had seen all these board-rooms, mess halls, berths, wardrooms, tailor shop, narrow halls and watertight hatches countless times in movies and on television. There were no real surprises except for the headroom. I don't recall John Wayne or Gregory Peck ducking under every doorway as they walked or raced down companionways. Maybe they were shorter than they appeared on the screen? After about an hour of looking around the interior we headed up to the flight deck and the airplanes. The deck was so large it felt like you were on a runway at the airport, except you were at least five stories up in the air. The deck was covered with dozens of aircraft - jets, propeller planes and helicopters - and it wasn't crowded in the slightest. A big surprise was the relative small size of the fighter jets that flew from its deck. I have seen fighters up close before and they always seemed big. These planes were small by comparison and there were many that you could walk up to and peer into the cockpit without having to stand on a ladder.

We discovered we were overlooking a park across a stretch of harbour and could see a large bronze statue of that famous *Life* magazine photo of a sailor kissing a woman in New York at the end of the Second World War. We could also see a couple of America's Cup yachts cavorting in the waves. It was quite a spectacular view.

During our tour the ship had also been hosting some sort of catered event but The Midway was so big you barely noticed. In fact we didn't and ended up trying to access a stairway that we shouldn't. A couple of retired servicemen politely but firmly suggested we not continue the way we were going and pointed out where we should go instead. It didn't appear they wanted to have any discussion about it either.

We made our way out by pushing through the throngs and agreed that the visit had been well worth the risk of alienating retired servicemen with our inability to follow posted rules. We headed back the way we had come and opted to walk down the waterfront along its wide promenade. The crowds of people were still about but they were not overpowering so we had a leisurely stroll past a number of moored sailing ships and a couple of old submarines. Each was ready and able to pick our pockets for admission fees if we were interested in going aboard. We weren't but it was nice to see them from the shore.

As usual we were hungry and were closely watching for a place to eat but had not been impressed with the quality nor prices of the restaurants along the walkway. Fortunately the other side of the road from the water was festooned with stand alone restaurants and hotels. We espied an Elephant and Castle and as we recognized the name and had enjoyed a meal at a sister restaurant in Toronto at the beginning of our journey we decided that was the place for us. We had lunch and a glass of beer while enjoying just sitting down. Refreshed we once again walked about with the crowds enjoying the day until we mutually agreed that was it. Since we knew where we were in relation to the train station we headed that way looking for a cab and our next thrill ride.

ALONG THE HARBOUR PROMENADE

Throughout the day we had marveled at how rich the city and its citizens appeared to be, but we did seem to see a large number of homeless people. There were way too many people walking about talking to themselves for my way of thinking. Undoubtedly the pleasant climate is attractive to all including those down on their luck.

It was late afternoon when we got back to the hotel and we took the opportunity to walk down the road towards Old Town. One of our maps indicated an Irish place called, appropriately enough, Kelly's Pub. It seemed close by on the map so we were considering it as a place to dine. It was only a few blocks and once there we found a small building with absolutely no windows and when we stuck our heads inside, no surprise, it seemed quite dark. The menu posted on the outside wall was nothing to write home about and I suggested to Gary the place reminded me of the kind of place where you fight your way in and then later fight your way out. Not that there was anything wrong with that; it was just that I have lost all desire for that type of dining experience in my middle age. Gary concurred and suggested we might do well to check with the hotel front desk for advice.

SAN DIEGO SKYLINE ACROSS FROM THE WATERFRONT

We did and the kid at the desk was most helpful. We started out by saying what we were considering and his face made a sudden and what I assumed to be an involuntary grimace at the mention of Kelly's Pub. Without saying anything negative about the place he quickly whipped out one of those tourist type maps. He pointed out that less than two blocks further along from Kelly's was Old

Town where at least two dozen restaurants and bars could be found that he suggested would be more conducive to pleasant dining. He also said it was a safe walk which put our minds at rest as that is something always at the forefront of any traveler thoughts.

What is that phrase? The best laid plans of mice and men....

By the time we were set to go it was chucking down rain. The first rain we'd seen since leaving Toronto and it was like walking through a bucket of water. The three-storey wing of our hotel was separated from the main building by a large patio with an outdoor hot tub and a couple of patio sets for guests to enjoy the outdoors. It was raining so hard you could barely see your hand in front of your face and by time we got to the other building we were soaked through. Discretion being the better part of valour we decided we needed an alternative to walking to a restaurant. The hotel had a small shop which carried packaged meals and sandwiches so we decided to eat in. Again remembering a frightful experiences with packaged sandwiches in England I opted for a chef's salad that turned out to be quite pleasant. Gary had clearly forgotten the English experience.

It strikes me now as odd that we never considered a cab to a restaurant. We had no difficulty calling cabs, notwithstanding some trepidation around the quality of the local cab drivers. Likely we were more worn out than we thought and the rain was a reasonable excuse to have a night in. We watched television for a while and had the usual (brandy) as the rain continued to pound down until after 10:00pm. It would have been quite dreary if we had opted to head out but it turned out to be a nice end to a terrific day.

Not so fast. Around 3:00am we were awakened to the sound of somebody pounding on a door somewhere in the hall shouting "Police" in a quite authoritative voice. I got up to have a look out the window. I can't imagine why I would have expected to see anything on the freeway outside the window and of course saw nowt. Since I was up anyway I went to the bathroom and while so employed considered that since it seemed to come from the hallway and we had heard nothing else it must have been some sort of gag. Convincing myself it was so I went back to bed and dozed fitfully for a little while thinking about home before finally falling back asleep.

November 21, Monday

By 8:00am the sky out over the Pacific Ocean was clear and blue. Just like the hotel in Albuquerque we had a nice breakfast provided in a common room. This room was not as pleasant as the previous and it likely doubled as a meeting room. In Albuquerque the sitting area had a fireplace with a television and the space was available all day. Here the tables and chairs were set up conference room style with the buffet on wheeled carts lined alongside the wall and everything was removed after breakfast. But it was free and there was plenty to eat.

The plan was to head to Old Town and spend the day meandering about doing the tourist thing. By 10:00am we were on our way down the same road we traversed when Kelly's Pub was discovered and sure enough two blocks beyond we were in the Old Town where we stopped at a little coffee shop almost immediately. I had to use the bathroom and being Canadian felt it would be inappropriate to use their facilities if we didn't spend any money. We sat at a small table on the pavement and watched life go by with me sipping tea and Gary getting his daily jolt of espresso. By now it had only just gone eleven and already many were out and about. Viewing the people walking and the cars passing it was clear we were in a fashionable and upscale area. All in all it was quite pleasant to sit surrounded by trees with flowers perfuming the air and watch the world flow by.

This Old Town was much larger than Albuquerque's and seemed more developed and diverse. Albuquerque's had been populated with small independent shops and a few restaurants all within a six block square area. San Diego's seemed twice as big with dozens of restaurants and a much larger number of independent shops; on balance the place seemed more trendy and tourist centric. A number of older buildings had been reconstructed to period times and there were also a number of museums. While both towns seemed of similar age it was it was interesting that Albuquerque Old Town seemed to have a greater Mexican influence on its buildings.

We of course picked up a little history of Old Town San Diego. A long since dried up river had once run alongside the site on its meander through Mission Valley to the ocean. Kumeyaay Indians had prospered beside the river for thousands of years. In 1542 explorer Jan Rodiquez Cabrillo chanced upon the area whereupon it was promptly forgotten about. I should say the white man forgot about it as the Native Americans still knew it was there. In 1602, while mapping what would become the California coast, Sebastian Vizcaino rediscovered the spot and named it San Diego de Alcala. Not much really happened as a result of that until the early 1700s when Russian explorers started claiming lands on the west coast of North America. I must say that in spite of a lifelong study and love of history I had no knowledge of Russian explorers reaching that far down the coast of North America. Anyway, the Russian interlopers upset the King of Spain, whose advisors felt that the faraway lands were rich in gold. In response he ordered a number of expeditions to support Spain's claims over the territory.

One expedition led by Gaspar de Portola consisted of the expected soldiers and missionaries but also included tradesmen to help establish outposts. They embarked from Mexico and landed at the bay of San Diego in 1769 and were met on the beach by the friendly First Nations peoples. Things didn't stay friendly for long but by that time it was already far too late for the First Nations. In keeping with the European style Father Junipero Serra immediately convened a mass and a military post was established on Presidio Hill. From this first step would develop the 21 missions under the direction of Serra, which became the cornerstone of California's colonization. This transpired some 60 years after Albuquerque's founding by the way.

Thus began the Spanish period and when Mexico gained independence from Spain in 1821 a new military command arrived in San Diego. The settlement now consisted of the mission and a garrison which serviced the port ten kilometres away with the bulk of the labour area's force made up of Kumeyaay Indians. Naturally some saw a future in the new town and a number of soldiers began to build homes below Presidio Hill. These first handful of homes were built around the still existing open plaza and would become the nucleus of the community. Two of the homes built in 1827 alongside the plaza are still standing. This plaza was likely three times larger than Albuquerque's and gave the place a much more open and expansive feel.

While San Diego was a Mexican possession the community was wide open and Americans and other visitors enjoyed the town's fiestas and bull fights. This was all to end in 1846 when the United States declared war on Mexico and the American story of San Diego began. Following the war's end in 1849 Californians wrote their constitution, and the area became a state in 1850 with San Diego incorporated as a city shortly after. The next 20 years were tough. The gradual decline of a military presence caused the small community to become insular from the outside world and making matters worse were a never-ending series of natural disasters. Wild fires, storms that generated flooding high tides, an earthquake in 1862, plus several years of drought and a smallpox epidemic all combined to decimate the region.

Things were pretty bleak in 1868 when San Franciscan Alonzo Horton arrived on the scene and decided the town would be better off located closer to the sea. Construction of "New Town" soon followed and a number of retail and civic buildings were already up and running a year later when gold was discovered in nearby Julian. This created a need for goods and services for the gold hunters and a boom jumpstarted New Town. It was only a matter of time before the old settlement was eclipsed. Time passed and more government offices moved to the new area which only encouraged existing businesses to follow suit. The final nail was driven in 1872 when fire once again consumed a number of buildings in Old Town this time engulfing the court house.

All was not lost for Old Town though. In 1907 a local sugar industry magnate began purchasing buildings and started a revival and a renewed interest in the Spanish and Mexican beginnings. At the same time the dawn of the automobile age was greatly increasing tourism. By the 1930s buildings were being constructed in the "Spanish" style and in 1968 Old Town San Diego became a State Historical Park. The rediscovery and preservation of the area was complete.

But it was now lunch time. We had passed a number of restaurants as we had made our way to the centre of Old Town and one had caught our eye. Originally it was a stately residence with a large veranda spanning the entire front of the building. A number of interior walls had been removed to create a dining room and bar and though it had lots of windows it seemed dark, likely due to the overhanging veranda. It also had a beer advertisement of a comely blonde holding a Bud that seemed to catch my eye. The front yard still had an old ornamental wrought iron fence separating the property from the street but the grass lawn had been paved over and was set with tables and chairs for al fresco dining. It was a beautiful sunny warm day so we decided to eat outside. We enjoyed a local craft beer that I don't recall the name of and I had a shrimp burrito. It was another huge meal and it was getting to the point where I thought I should start watching. It seemed that since we left Toronto meal portions had been steadily increasing while prices went the other way.

We felt good enough after lunch to wander about for another hour and a half and then meandered our way home. Aside from a bag of candy we didn't spend much else over the course of the day. Our tourist aspirations no longer required trinkets to remind us or - is that prove? - we had been somewhere. That was not to say we didn't continue to purchase supplies. My nail clippers gave up the ghost on the train so I bought a new pair (why is it called a pair?) and more importantly we were running low on brandy yet again. We purchased another bottle with no concerns from Gary around budget or country of origin this time.

In spite of never buying anything I found I was out of cash again so when we got back to the hotel I hit the ATM in the lobby before stopping by the front desk to make arrangements for a ride to the train station the next morning. We were told the shuttle ran every 20 minutes "or so" with the train station the first stop before it travelled on to the airport. The clerk reckoned that we should take the 5:20am shuttle so a 4:15 wakeup call was arranged. Ever since a night in Toulouse when Lynn and I had depended on an early wakeup call that never arrived I have been tentative around trusting in them. Accordingly that night I set my watch alarm plus my Grundig portable radio alarm and Gary also set his alarm clock. We felt reasonably assured that one of them was bound to wake us.

But that was in the future. In the meantime we decided to have a coffee on the outside patio so Gary could smoke a cigar. The traffic on the freeway on the other side of the retaining wall was nonstop and bumper to bumper in both directions. Vehicles were truly barreling along at what looked like 120 km/h, yet within the hour when rush hour was at its peak speeds had slowed to under 50 km/h and at times it stopped completely dead. It was quite something and I could readily see why driving in such a lemming-like condition could cause a person to snap into road rage. While sitting out on the patio we realized this was our last night in a hotel and there would be no more cabs after tomorrow and, more importantly, there was only one more train ride to enjoy. Well, to be accurate there were two as we had to change trains in Los Angeles but you get my drift. Back in the room I decided to have a quick shower and the sun totally set in the 10 minutes I was in the bathroom, on the train you'll recall it took an hour and a half to set.

Our waitress at lunch in Old Town had suggested that we should take a meal at a place we had passed a couple of times called Crazee Burger and we decided to give it a go. We considered that if she offered up somewhere other than where she worked it was likely a decent spot. Surprising and for the second time in a very short period Gary once again played against type around meal times. We headed out just after 8:00pm for the enjoyable walk down the now familiar road. I kept quiet but this breaking of long ingrained practice around fixed meal times was disconcerting. Were these subtle changes to type designed to keep me just slightly off balance and could I really depend on him to plan meals?

We passed a garden encroaching on the street that was full of bird of paradise plants and another with a tree blooming with dark purple flowers, and the fragrance in the air once again reminded me of Mexico. Back home we would only see such in flower shops, especially in November. The walk to the restaurant only took a half an hour and as we had nothing but time we read the outdoor posted menu, whereupon we discovered that the joint had been featured on my favourite Food Channel television show, *Dinners, Diners and Dives*. This sealed the deal.

We ordered at the counter and paid pending delivery to our table. When I whipped out my Visa card the guy at the counter said we must be Canadian. I had no idea and was slightly dumbfounded for a second or two. It turned out that he recognized the CIBC symbol on my card. He was originally from London, Ontario and his family had moved to San Francisco when he was young although not so young that he forgot the CIBC logo. He had come to San Diego eight years previous to go to university and while he never did finish school he decided to stay on. I am always amazed at how people whose employment clearly cannot be well-paying seem to be able to make a life in such expensive cities. I was also struck again by the number of connections one runs across in life from seemingly the most tenuous coincidences. We had passed this restaurant at least three times in the previous days and had not given it any thought. Then a cute little waitress from another restaurant recommended it and the night we go our server is from Canada who takes the time to acknowledge it to two strangers in a strange land.

We each had a huge hamburger and I enjoyed a Mexican beer which I had now grown quite fond of. We didn't stay out too late as we had an early train to catch but back at the hotel we did have the usual while watching a little television and discussing highlights of the trip. Later when firing up Gary's Playbook for our daily fix of life back home I discovered Neil had sent an email. He hoped we were enjoying the weather in San Diego because it was horrible where we were headed. It turned out that we had nothing really to fear or worry about as the weather in the great northwest was about to change for the better. At least it would for the short duration of our visit and that really was all that mattered to the selfish travelers we were.

MAGNIFICENT TREE IN OLD TOWN COURT YARD

It had been another great couple of days but we were both looking forward to getting back on the train. The train was the thing. While the stops along the way were terrific we both considered that if we had only spent a day or two at each location it would have been just as enjoyable. If I were to do it again I would arrange a few more overnight stops along the way and definitely set my alarm while onboard so that I didn't sleep through so many stations. We had slept right through most of Arizona, not to mention Dodge City. That evening we also spent time talking about train travel in general. In our experience we lost all track of time when we were riding the rails and we were never bored. In fact time just breezed by and we both had trouble recalling how long any particular piece of the journey had taken.

November 22, Tuesday – heading for Portland on The Pacific Surfliner and The Coast Starline

Considering all the alarms we set and the wakeup call that rang promptly it should be of no surprise that we were up at a quarter to five. We watched the news on CNN while packing and saw a piece about police pepper spraying students staging a sit-in at the University of Davis. Here was another connection. Neil left Winnipeg to study at the U of Davis 35 years ago. I had not thought nor can recall even hearing of that university in dozens of years and here on the day I'm heading out to visit him his alma matter is out in front on the news, although not in a pleasant way.

There was also another piece on the news. The item after the police at an American University pepper spraying a peaceful student sit-in was about somebody setting off tear gas in the South Korean Parliament. The local newscasters made a number of jokes about the type of world the Koreans live in where there would be this type of outrage in their Parliament. They had nary a comment nor opinion about armed police pepper spraying unarmed students sitting on the grass in a common area of an American university. Funny that.

San Diego to Portland

By 5:20am we were sitting in the San Diego train station. There had only been two others on the shuttle and they were headed to the airport. I settled down and Gary wandered off to find a bathroom and something to eat. While he was gone I people watched the crowd of about a dozen. I started singing part of a Simon and Garfunkel tune to myself, *"sitting in a railway station, got a ticket for my destination"* and realized I was absolutely comfortable and completely happy.

The station, like most we had been in over the balance of the trip, looked to be close to 100 years old. It was also a fair size. It was actually a terminus since the rail line ended or began here, depending on whether you were coming or going. The grand hall had yellow-painted tile walls and was two stories high with an open ceiling supported by massive wooden beams; travelers rested on comfortable old bum-worn wooden benches. Gary had by now returned so I too went off to find the bathroom but found it locked for cleaning. Why it needed to be cleaned so close to the departure of the first train of the day was a puzzlement and would remain a mystery.

Despite knowing what we needed to know Gary went off to double check with the ticket agent.... "boarding outside on the platform at 6:00am, please line up orderly." The line-up on the platform was short and while still very early in the morning you could sense it was going to be a beautiful day. Just as the train was leaving San Diego the conductor told us we could move down to the lower level if we wished but we decided not to. The next day while shooting the breeze as an Oregon breeze was shooting by the window it crossed our minds that sitting in the lower level might have been an upgrade offer that we overlooked.

SAN DIEGO STATION

We were well on our way by 7:45am and by then had stopped at numerous stations picking up commuters destined for Los Angeles and area. We'd had no difficulty finding seats when we boarded but now the car was packed and it would get ever more crowded as we neared our destination. There seemed to be a dozen folks getting on at every stop with none getting off. And what a difference out the train window from the first part of our journey 10 days back! Then it had been miles of abandoned buildings and worn out homes - now it was miles of mansions and rich apartment buildings. Here were all the trappings of unqualified success plus palm trees - but with a dark underside; we noticed a man sleeping under a bridge not 30 metres from a boat yard and marina filled to capacity with what could only be called yachts.

As we moved ever nearer Los Angeles the California car culture was constantly outside the other side of the window. Multi lane, multilevel freeways everywhere like something out of a science fiction movie depicting a future world, *Blade Runner* perhaps, only our views were all sunshine and light not dark and foreboding. It was impressive and overpowering and I wondered at the enormous building challenge and expense of it all. Amazingly, the bulk of these fantastic byways had all been designed, developed and constructed in my lifetime. It wasn't just the packed freeways either, for there were dealer lots and parking lots everywhere and of course the two or three vehicles in each and every driveway. Never mind a chicken in every pot.

There seemed to be a clear dividing line between the wealthy and the poor along this route rather than the more gradual shift we had seen on the ride out from Buffalo. It was around Irvine that we began to notice the beginnings of trailer parks and razor wire atop fences surrounding businesses and more disturbingly around homes and apartment buildings. Perhaps poor people and criminals were not allowed south of Irvine? Likely the higher population density brought with it a higher level of poverty and crime. In any event seeing so much razor wire did take the colour out of the California rose. Near Santa Ana we started to see nice middle class townhomes built right up against the rail line. It must have been really noisy with trains going by every quarter of an hour.

I was a little bored and found that I was listening to a conversation directly behind me between two kids of about 14 discussing the benefits and names of Care Bears. I have some solid knowledge of Care Bears as my daughters spent a number of years enamoured of these soft and cuddly toys and had acquired a substantial sloth. (I'll bet you didn't know that's what a group of bears is called – I didn't either until I Googled it). This bear collection was a result of being spoiled rotten by parents, grandparents, aunts and uncles alike. My kids are both just in their 30s now so Care Bears must be making a comeback. The thing was that I am sure my darling children were done with them by time they were 10 or 11 and the two behind me were clearly older than that.

At 8:25am we pulled into Fullerton for the second time - where Gary and I had disembarked from The Southwest Chief a few days previous. No more backtracking, it was all new territory for us now. Fullerton seemed like a nice place covered as it was with palm trees and towering red flowering hedges that everyone seemed to have surrounding their properties. The train was now well and truly full of commuters and every five minutes or so we would stop and more would cram on board. The poor buggers were headed in to work I guess.

THE CONCRETE CHANNELED AND NEARLY DRY LOS ANGELES RIVER

By mid-morning we were nearing Los Angeles proper with the train still packed. We had passed over concrete river channels a number of times. These huge concrete channels had been constructed over the past century to properly direct the southern California waterways. The inconvenient routes that nature had determined were not at all good enough for people who knew best so the courses of natural channels were changed to something more acceptable. Today the channels were dry, perhaps there was a drought. Perhaps the long-held belief by many that the overuse of water had finally resulted in the strange sight of waterways running out of water long before they reached the Pacific. Or perhaps Mother Nature was teaching people not to mess with things beyond their control. The channels did bear evidence of flash flooding with great clumps of detritus scattered hither and yon and deposited no doubt by fast high-running water. One spot looked to me like where Governor Arnold rode his motorcycle while being chased by the semi truck in one of the *Terminator* movies.

I also saw the Hollywood sign up in the hills and that was a great treat.

We rolled into the Los Angeles station on track nine then walked with the throngs through a wide tunnel to the waiting room. Both the tunnel and waiting room were readily recognizable from television and movies. In fact a few months later I was watching a cop show with my Erin and a scene was shot pretty well from the exact place where Gary and I had sat down while awaiting our connection. I could tell it was the same spot by the view of a book and newspaper stand way off in another corner where Gary had gone searching for a *Wall Street Journal*.

Our wait stop was only 40 minutes, not much time allotted to one of the greatest cities in the world but we had no regrets. We sat and watched the passing travelers and with no real surprise noticed a couple of homeless folks trying to be invisible. It felt great sitting beside an open window in that grand hall full of people with a gentle fragrant breeze wafting in. The breeze coming in was almost perfumed enough to overpower the smell of urine that was invading our space, almost perfumed enough. Forty minutes here just might have been enough.

Later with no sense of urgency we leisurely walked back down the tunnel to track ten. Maybe we were savouring the pleasure of boarding the last train of our adventure. Whatever the reason it was a delightful experience to be boarding a train at the Los Angeles Union Station. I had a slight sense of sorrow mingled with the anticipation of the ride to meet my old friend at the Portland end of our train ride.

Just like the trip from Albuquerque when we disembarked early at Fullerton and saved some time on the way to San Diego, we could have saved some time on this leg. If we had acted on known information we could have gotten off at Albany rather than Portland. Portland was an hour and a half from Corvallis while Albany was only a half an hour away. If we had gone that route we would have saved ourselves a lot of waiting in Portland and saved Neil being stuck in traffic on a holiday evening. However, we would have missed out on a great meal in Portland, but I am getting ahead of myself again.

We stepped up into our carriage with an unseemly entitlement that we had somehow acquired. We were sleeping car folk and as such were special which was ably reinforced by the porter providing each of us with a small bottle of champagne in our compartment. The plonk was welcomed and quickly enjoyed but we had bigger fish to fry as we had an important decision to make. This final carriage was of the same type we had boarded so long ago in Kansas City, which meant no upper berth window to allow the occupant to watch the world go by from bed. This I grant seems like a small luxury but it was one I had come to enjoy before and after sleep.

But I was torn. I do enjoy my sleep and the upper had a one-piece mattress while the lower was put together with four cushions. Much like the story of the princess and the pea, I could feel the cracks between the cushions and they interfered with a good night's sleep. It was my option to have the lower berth with the window and a decision was still pending.

That aside, we were in for a famous treat. The Coast Starlight had the only refurbished 1950s era parlour car on the entire Amtrak system and it was available only to us sleeper car people. The car reputedly provided better meals than the diner plus there was a wine tasting evening scheduled. All this would only help to increase our sense of entitlement. This is the only way to travel. Later after the holiday I saw an episode of *The Big Bang Theory* where the characters were on this line and Sheldon spoke glowingly of this very parlour car.

Once underway we quickly settled back into the routine of life on the train and the schedule, which revolved around meal reservations. It wasn't that we spent our time waiting on dinner; rather we seemed to use meals to measure and separate the day. It also made little difference when not dining where we sat - club car, parlour car or compartment - the view of the world outside was wonderful. When we'd had enough of one place we moved onto the next and its different perspective. If you had enough of looking out the window you could read or solve some world problem over a drink. We had not a care in the world.

While travelling past Burbank, readily identifiable by a huge white sign on a hill that read "Burbank" as in "beautiful downtown Burbank" from the old *Tonight Show* I noticed dozens of airplane vapour trails in the sky. These were doubtless from the countless airplanes ferrying people in a hurry in and out of LAX airport. Back home if you see two vapour trails at any given time it seems a lot. We were also keenly aware of oil wells slowly pumping black gold out of the ground. They seemed to be everywhere, countryside, ranches, cities, and even people's backyards. The pumps looked like those bird toys we had as kids that perched on the side of glasses bobbing up and down as if they were drinking the water.

Unhappily, there was bit of bother on this train. Our compartment was on the right side which was in fact the wrong side. Not to be confusing but we were on the right side of a train heading north. Since Buffalo, being on the right side hadn't been a problem but the Pacific was now on our left. Out our window we had a nice view of the countryside but it wasn't the Pacific. Fortunately, the compartment opposite was not occupied and with both doors open we could easily see the ocean. Notwithstanding my earlier comments around compartment doors letting you know when they weren't latched properly, we would manage to cope and there was always the club car where we could get all the view we needed. Still it would have been nice to have been on the right side of the carriage, I mean left.

Most of the trip along the seaside offered views of passing freighters, fishing vessels and oil drilling platforms just out to sea. There were dozens of platforms over the course of a few hours and one or two were always in view. I had no idea that oil was drilled offshore of California. I knew about the Gulf Coast, the North Sea and of course off the coast of Newfoundland but had absolutely no awareness that they drilled for oil here. Just like the brussel sprouts in Kansas City and Russian explorers I was to learn something new this day. Travel is an education, isn't it?

PACIFIC OCEAN VIEWS, NORTH OF LOS ANGELES

It was soon time to eat and our luncheon companions were a woman and her grown son on their way to Seattle and then a visit to Corvallis. I'll admit by this time I was no longer surprised by a world filled with coincidences. What were the chances of us having lunch on a train heading from Los Angeles with a couple who were going to the same place we were headed? Keep in mind that Corvallis was not a station stop along the way.

During the meal we passed through Oxnard and miles and miles of vegetable and strawberry fields. We were also beginning to see grape vines everywhere. Fields and fields of them and many covered with half moon shaped plastic enclosures. The enclosures kept heat in, frost off and bugs out I guessed. It did look odd and like our earlier view of irrigated wheat fields it must be a very expensive way to farm. Out the other side we could see oil rigs in the Santa Barbara Channel that looked to be no longer pumping.

As we were nearing Vandenberg Air Force Base an announcement over the intercom provided a history of this important base, which takes up an incredible amount of California coast line - we would travel through it for nearly an hour. The land was a brown rolling hilly sort with the occasional gravel road running off to the horizon. There were also huge isolated buildings dotting the landscape. I found it interesting that while we spent nearly an hour traversing this gigantic base we never saw any evidence of life: not a soul was seen, not a truck or car, no evidence of life at all. It was eerie.

We learned that Vandenberg Air Force Base in addition to being an air base was also the site of a number of other things. Like the launching sites of Titan missiles aimed west out over the Pacific and also northward in the event of an attack on the U.S. I wondered if in the event of such an attack would consideration be given to the interception and blowing up of incoming missiles over Canada, that was just purely rhetorical. On a less fearsome note the now retired space shuttle could have used this base for launch or for a landing site in the event of inclement weather on a return journey. It had never been used as such but we saw a hanger that could be utilized for this purpose, and also what we believed to be some Titan missile silos. While these buildings were some distance from the train they clearly were enormous structures. Oh, and they announced that cell phone service was blocked for security reasons during passage through the area. This last item did not bother two thrifty Canadian travelers who had no intention of paying roaming charges unless their lives depended on it and only then if there was a guarantee their lives would be spared by using them.

Apparently security had been much tighter in the 1960s when the base was considered a classified zone. In those days Military Police boarded the train at the boundary of the base to shroud all the train windows from the outside and an MP was stationed in each carriage while the train traversed the base. A couple of trains went each way every day along this rail line from Los Angeles to San Francisco so the logistics and costs of such procedures must have been horrendous. It is amazing in hindsight what steps the American government thought were required to protect its citizens from themselves during the heady days of the Cold War. I am not sure that they think those days are behind us yet.

I have no difficulty with the concept of national security but I do have a problem with the concept that some citizens have a right to know more about my country than I do. Or that there are some who are deemed better able to be entrusted with information because they somehow would make better use of it than the great unwashed. You don't have to look too far to see how quickly and easily information has been turned on its citizens. Such blatant situations like having windows covered and armed guards in a railway car as it passes for an hour through land in a country that claims to be the freest in the world gives rise to thoughts of a police and not a free state. Not to mention that continuing to this day in blocking cell phone coverage on a train travelling 100 km/h seems mildly paranoid.

After successfully traversing the military base without incident we investigated the amenities of the 1950s parlour car.

We discovered the lounge was on the second level as expected but there was also a lower level which had a movie theatre that screened films twice nightly. A very nice option for some I imagine but we had no interest in a movie whilst on board. A wine tasting was another matter. The event was scheduled for 3:00pm and reservations were required. We booked ours' before the attendant had finished telling us we needed them. We also decided that we should take our evening meal in the parlour car as the posted meals seemed nicer than those in the dining car. Reservations for 5:15pm were promptly made and this time it was me who was already extremely hungry.

While it may seem that I constantly go on about Gary's fastidiousness around meal times I am not one to miss a meal if it can be helped. Like my daughter Sara I can become quite surly if not fed and watered in a timely fashion.

There were only four booths available in the car and we had expected reservations would go quickly but we had no difficulty at all in making them. We were even more surprised to have no difficulty making arrangements for the wine tasting. We were sure there would be a rush for seats if for no other reason than it was something new to do. I still don't understand why our fellow sleeping car travelers did not jump at the chance to at least take advantage of the car for meals. It wasn't that they were unaware of the offer since you had to pass through it to get to the diner. Up front the great masses in coach likely didn't even have knowledge of the parlour car as access was effectively blocked and denied by the regular dining car.

We arrived at the wine tasting just before three and found the attendant already dispensing the first glass. There were four Oregon wines on offer none of which either of us had tasted before. I enjoyed them all and would have been hard pressed to identify a winner. We also enjoyed a modest selection of Oregon cheese and crackers with the wine; all in all it was a nice way to while away an hour. To try to recoup some of the costs of the free event the attendant offered up some advertising materials for sale as remembrances. Gary bought a wine glass embossed with The Coast Starlight logo, a uniformed and capped attendant with a towel draped over his left arm set against a back drop of a mountain range; all very art deco-ish. I opted for a coffee mug with the same design. There was an added bonus in these purchases as Gary got a free glass of wine with dinner and I a free hot chocolate.

The meal experience was not really much different than the dining car other than fewer companions and absolutely no pressure to depart. Just as dinner was ending we rode into Salinas and I started humming *Me and Bobbi McGee*. You'll recall my mentioning Gary blurting out "Salinas" in his sleep in Kansas City but I didn't notice that passing through the town even registered with him.

Later over the nightly brandy we found ourselves reflecting yet again on how even with what at the time seemed staggering setbacks we'd both had very lucky lives. These thoughts were doubtless germinated during conversations with fellow passengers who clearly had not enjoyed the same measure of employment happiness that we'd each had. I'm fairly certain that my children's generation will not be as fortunate as mine and I also think that this problem, if it is a problem, seems to have already impacted my American contemporaries. Many people we came across never knew the luxury of not having to worry about the next paycheque whereas we had always known at the back of our minds that, if we wanted, we had jobs for life. This knowledge afforded an enormous comfort and freedom I am now very grateful for.

While we'd both had complaints and troubles over the years it was clear that being brought up in Canada greatly enhanced our life opportunities. Make no mistake, we each took advantage of opportunities that came our way but it remains we were brought up in an environment that provided many opportunities and we were in a position to chase them down. Many of the folks we met over the course of the trip appeared not to have had the opportunities we did.

It turned out to be another terrific day of watching the world go by. The sky was clear and bright all day long and the blue Pacific was always in view. I won the bottom berth on a coin toss and was happy for the luxury of looking out the window from the lumpy bed on the last night on the train.

November 23, Wednesday

It was a good thing I had the lower berth. I must have drunk too much as I kept getting up to go to the bathroom all night long. By 8:00am we were in Oregon and miles from the coast with lots more train traffic going past. We wouldn't be seeing the Pacific again until we flew into Vancouver. The view out the window reminded me of Thunder Bay, only the trees and mountains were twice as big. When we'd gone to sleep we were on the only rail line now there were rails to the left and right of us and the passing train of choice seemed to be the legendary Union Pacific. We travelled through foothills for most of the morning but it slowly and continuously turned more mountainous as the hours passed and the weather turned colder. Not that we could tell it was cold from the comfort of the train but there was snow showing up in shaded areas.

Our breakfast companions this last day had boarded the previous evening at Emeryville, which was the closest Amtrak station to San Francisco. We had not noticed nor even been aware we were passing by the famous city and it likely would not have made much difference to us anyway. Generally we were blissfully unaware of any stop on the line unless we were disembarking. We were likely toasting the day at the time and so would have barely even noticed the stop.

We of course opted for breakfast in the parlour car. We both preferred its vintage style over the somewhat tacky 70s decor of the dining car, and being children of the '50s likely had something to do with that. Our breakfast companions were on their way to visit a daughter in Eugene which was just three stops before our own end of the line. The couple both taught in the engineering department at the University of Berkeley and they happily recounted a 2005 conference they attended in Ottawa. They had taken the train through Canada for their return journey and remembered stopping in Winnipeg though didn't recall Thunder Bay.

During breakfast we had been stopped for nearly an hour at a siding in Kalmuth Falls, the first Oregon station. Being stopped at a siding suggested that once again we were travelling on the only rail line and were moving back into the hinterland. The crew provided newspapers for passengers to pass the time while sidelined and the Kalmuth Falls Herald News predicted a rainy day and a high only reaching 42F, or 6C where we came from. In a moment of quiet while scanning the paper and a small map I marveled at the extent of the country we had traversed in such a relatively short time. By the time we returned to our respective homes we would have travelled a fairly loose circle of nearly 6,000 km. When I later looked at our route with the aid of my *National Geographic World Atlas* (the one I annoy family and friends by referring to it as the world's greatest atlas) I was amazed to see how much ground we had covered.

When once underway the view on both sides of the train was of scrubby hills with every spectrum of brown in sight, the only break in colour being the green of the pines. There were now only six hours or so left on the train and while we were looking forward to the next stage of the journey we both were sorry to see the ride ending. Every mile of the journey had been great and neither of us could think of any problem encountered that had in any way diminished our enjoyment of the train. Undoubtedly our being of similar natures when travelling certainly helped. It wasn't that we put up with things that annoyed us; it was that we just accepted what was put in front of us with good humour. On any trip away from regular life there will be unfamiliar situations that can quickly put a damper on things if you let them. Train travel is not all a bed of roses and like any experience outside of what you're used to it can be trying. We tried not to worry about or let things get to us that were beyond our control - and we had encountered plenty that was beyond our control.

The main thing with getting anywhere is that pretty much everything is completely beyond your control so it's best to sit back and let things happen when and as they will. Like spending half a day in the tiny Depew station on the outskirts of Buffalo awaiting a train from New York that seemed like it never would arrive. In your heart you know it had to show up some time since it was after all on its daily trip across the country. But still, where the hell was it? Like sitting on a siding in the middle of nowhere awaiting the passing of some nonexistent freight or being stopped dead on the tracks in Arizona because of a brake problem. Like traversing the transition space between carriages and thinking maybe one should just jump for it. Like standing in line waiting to order a beer whilst three ex-convicts discuss the various pluses and minuses of penitentiaries in the tri-state area. All you can do is find the comedy in the thing and enjoy the experience. There is absolutely nothing you can do about anything and since you have no control fretting will be of no benefit to yourself or your travelling companions. Getting flustered or even angry can't change anything except to spoil whatever comes next. Best to look at everything encountered as part of the experience. Having said all that, clearly, continental train travel should not be undertaken if schedules are fixed.

But there are multiple benefits to the train over flying. With the exception of the commuter train to and from San Diego passengers on our trains were of all ages just as on airlines but with clearly more children passengers on the rails. Likely cost is the most obvious reason for taking the family on the train in the U.S. but possibly it is also because train travel is less stressful than the rigmarole you go through getting on and off an airplane. The comfortably humane process of arriving for a train minutes before departure is especially delightful. There are similarities to the two modes of transport though; both are rife with late departures.

Another benefit of rail travel is that passengers are subjected to much less rolling and pitching when travelling. There are side to side movements to be sure but they are not nearly as abrupt as they can be on an airplane and especially at inconvenient moments. Other than gradual changes in elevation there is obviously little in the way of up and down motion to deal with on a train. While the bathrooms on both are similar in size their use on a train is also more comfortable. Any unexpected motion encountered when using the facilities on either can be bothersome but the train has the luxury of having no risk of a rapid downward movement that can re-teach the laws of gravity as it relates to water in the toilet you are perched on.

Then there are the meals. There is absolutely no comparison between actually sitting at a table to enjoy a meal and wolfing down something atop a drop leaf from a chair back six inches from your nose. Especially when you glance over and hope that the clearly uncomfortable person next to the window is not suddenly going to need to get to the toilet as you interminably gnaw on the piece of rubber chicken that was presented with great fanfare as the meal choice of the evening.

Canadians, certainly in the West, seldom even consider trains when making travel plans and pricing is undoubtedly the reason. Why pay nearly the same or even more when flying will get you there quicker, even if you arrive flustered and tired? Passenger train travel seems to be slowly dying away in Canada and if it does disappear it will because of cost. That will be sad because once the train is gone it will never be back and it really is a lovely way to travel.

Our train was now climbing ever higher and we had traversed a number of tunnels as we moved up to the higher elevations of the Rockies. We were deep within pine forests and the trees were really quite tall. The previous occasional bit of snow on the ground had now turned into regular sightings of snow banks alongside trees and in ditches. Then something odd happened. All of a sudden and even though we continued to climb the snow all but disappeared over the course of a few miles. It was very strange and clearly the temperature outside was now warmer but still cocooned as we were within the train we had no way of knowing. By noon we seemed to be heading downhill and the weather had changed to misty clouds. We were also seeing signs that we were close to civilization again. Homes, adjacent rail lines, highways and the like were now reappearing as part of the landscape out the windows.

OREGON, KIND OF LOOKS LIKE HOME EXCEPT FOR THE MOUNTAINS

It was along this stretch that we passed an interesting geographical feature. We had been travelling for some time alongside a shallow river with what looked like a very wide and well-washed channel. It was clear the water level had recently been much higher. We initially figured it might have been a tidal river, similar to the Tyne which empties into the North Sea near Newcastle. That tide goes upstream for nearly 16 kilometres. Clever fellows that we were we soon discounted the idea of a tidal river. First off, we must have been at least 160 kilometres from the Pacific; secondly and much more importantly we were up in the mountains. It would have had to be some tidal surge to reach up that high. No, we felt that more than likely this was a seasonally fierce running river that emptied into a lake. We also kicked around that perhaps there was a dam nearby. Ten minutes later we were proved right on the second. The river channel, which had been steadily widening, suddenly abutted a dam whose holding capacity was far from being reached. We never did discover why the water level was so low but the dammed up water was likely run off from the mountains and the present low level suggested massive needs of water downstream.

NOT IN CIVILIZATION ANY MORE

All this conversation and conjecture took place in our compartment and when the puzzle was finally solved we headed down to the parlour car for our last meal on the rails. Just as we were standing to move along for lunch a Union Pacific freight train barreled by outside our window. The freight train was hauling dozens of Canadian Pacific Railway, Government of Canada and Saskatchewan Pool grain cars. It reminded us of home and it felt good.

Today was the start of the American Thanksgiving holiday and since we had left Los Angeles there had been regular announcements from the dining car manager around how the train was full to capacity at 1,100 people. He claimed he had never seen so many people on a train in his quarter century of service and opined nobody could walk up and purchase a ticket at any station along the line because the train was full to capacity. At the end of his little discourse he announced that due to the huge numbers of people he was doubtful that even his crew could possibly serve meals in the dining car to all who wanted one. That is unless of course we booked reservations as quickly as possible and that we remembered to be on time for our bookings. It was the same announcement with each meal and invariably before the meal period was over he would come back on the intercom and tell passengers that room was still available at such and such a sitting. I think he was trying to manipulate us. Gary and I had no difficulty in getting meal times reserved nor did we experience any pressure to rush our meal. Either the catering manager was a worrywart, impressed by his own importance, just liked to hear himself talk or else passengers were just not hungry enough to pay through the nose for a meal.

In addition to the dining car supervisor's meal announcements the train conductor also made regular pronouncements. We assumed the reason was that the enormous numbers of passengers on board increased the stress on the crew to ensure smooth running of the train. His missives were around getting off the train at a station that was not your final destination to stretch your legs, which was undoubtedly a colloquialism for having a smoke. His tone was unmistakably a thinly-veiled threat and we had become used to his regular updates on the passage. The updates were so regular that it was impossible not to miss that the tone of each subsequent announcement was getting notably stronger.

Near Los Angeles the message had started out as a gentle reminder that if you got off you risked causing the train being late leaving the station. This soon morphed into perhaps the mighty

Coast Starlight could leave without you. Now in the great northwest the message was more dire and direct than the laid back Californian message had been. Here in Oregon the message was quite clear, get off the train and we will leave you behind, ergo, do not get off the train if it isn't your stop. During one announcement he mentioned that just the previous week they had left four poor hapless souls standing on the platform in Eugene and these dolts were undoubtedly left behind without benefit of luggage. As we neared the bustling metropolis of Albany the announcement reached its nadir and was as clear as it could possibly have been. "If you insist on getting off the train and this isn't your last stop it will become your last stop." This message was received loud and clear by a couple of bumbling Canadians.

Just before 2:00pm we were near Albany and closer to Corvallis and Neil than Portland was going to be. With better planning we would have been getting ready to depart but instead we watched the station go by and spent our time looking out at meadows and fields of sheep. Meanwhile, Neil was on the road to Portland.

The views immediately brought to mind the innumerable sheep pastures we traversed in the north of England on our tramp beside Hadrian's Wall. I acquired a taste for lamb and mutton on that trip. There had been three different types of sheep. Some had been all white, others white with black legs and faces and still others white with black legs. Gary and I had tramped through enough sheep-filled fields to be able to recognize the type of sheep in the pasture from the shape and smell of the recycled product the adorable creatures deposited with great verve and style. Out our window here the sheep all had black faces and legs, which if I recall rightly meant that they were raised for wool not for food. Happily on this trip we wouldn't get firsthand knowledge of sheep. But of cattle, that was to be a different matter.

An hour later we were close enough to Portland to realize that our rail holiday was nearing its end. I had started the trip with no trepidation but had expected some irritating moments. I had travelled by train a number of times in the past as a child and as an adult. There had always been something to spoil the trip; it was usually delays but I do recall one winter trip delayed because the steam pipes providing heat had frozen. You could have hung meat in that carriage. How cold does it have to be for a pipe full of steam to freeze? On reflection, any irritation caused by delays was due to boredom on my part. I can say that on this trip we were never bored, annoyed in Depew absolutely but never bored. In spite of, or perhaps because of no television or radio and armed with books, good conversation and a congenial travelling companion, time passed pleasantly and enjoyably. The passage was also greatly enhanced by the helpful and friendly rail staff and the meeting of new people over shared meals. These things all combined to make the ride on the rails comfortable with efficiency and humanity. We travelled with none of that sense that we were just baggage that air travel regularly imparts to its passengers.

As we approached the Portland area it reminded me of both Vancouver Island and Winnipeg. The geography was like the island and the vegetation was very similar to home. We pulled into the very small and very busy Portland station on time at 3:20pm. We started and ended the trip right on time!

Neil had arranged to meet us at the station and while he wasn't there we weren't unduly ruffled as we used the time waiting to decompress, collect our thoughts and watch the crowds. The front doors of the station were wide open and people were milling about everywhere. It was raining heavily but the temperature was quite pleasant. We sat around inside for a few minutes then reckoned that being outside might be as good idea as any. If we saw Neil drive up we could just jump in the car and he wouldn't have to park and then get soaking wet coming to get us. This would also avoid needlessly paying a parking tab. By 4:00pm in the gathering gloom we were beginning to have that first sense of misgiving and were glancing at the surrounding skyline for a nearby hotel - just in case you understand. There did seem to be a suitably attractive hotel sign just a couple of blocks away which information we filed without too much conversation.

I had yet to use my cell phone on this trip because of the near legendary roaming charges my provider levies in such circumstances but now thought this was as good a time as any to make a call. It transpired that Neil was stuck in traffic on the expressway. It was the night before Thanksgiving and he said he'd never seen such traffic but felt he was just 20 minutes away. Confidence restored, we found an unoccupied bench beneath the station awning and sat down to wait in comfort and satisfaction.

Then, just as I was physically and mentally relaxed, a drop of water fell directly on me. How do basketball players put it? Nothing but rim. This solitary drop, which by my calculation was an ounce of water, hit bare flesh on the back of my neck at damn near the middle of my shoulder blades. To be clear, it struck without touching hat, hair, coat collar or sweater and it was supercharged cold. I jumped near three feet in the air.

It eventually took Neil an hour to cover what normally would have taken a third of that time, but now that we had phone contact, albeit at a usurious rate, we weren't concerned. When he arrived he called out from his truck and we quickly jumped in. Over the many years Neil had lived in the U.S. I had only seen him half a dozen times but magically when we did get together it was always as though it had only been a few weeks since last we met. We immediately become the same couple of goofballs we were way back then, a time of no responsibilities without a care in the world. It happened again.

It was now fully dark and still chucking down rain. Our expected plan had been to stay the night at Neil's condo in Portland. But the best laid plans ...., again.

As he had done for the past 20 years Neil was preparing the Thanksgiving dinner the next day. He felt it best to head back the two hours to Corvallis despite having already been on the road for hours. Knowing then what we did I was sorry we hadn't heeded his earlier suggestion to get off the train in Albany. Since we were all hungry he suggested a brew pub in the downtown arts area for a meal. It was a nice place and the meal was very good but strangely the most memorable thing was the washroom. The restrooms were on the upper level which was crossed by way of a grating for a floor. This walkway was not directly over the diners below but you get the picture. It struck me that any woman wearing anything but jeans might have some trepidation wandering over this grate; at least they would in Winnipeg. I digress again as it was the men's room which was memorable.

I will try to be tasteful. Said washroom had been outfitted with recycled ancient fittings and the urinals of which there were three were gigantic. Each of these porcelain monoliths was fully two metres from floor to top and had wings, similar to a Queen Anne chair that shielded the user from prying eyes and cold northern winds. You didn't so much step up as step into the thing and the wings seemed to wrap quite round a person. To my left were a man and his son also taking advantage of the plumbing. The son appeared to be no more than four or five and as he stepped up he quite disappeared. It was almost as if he had stepped into a separate room or Dr. Who's Tardis.

Right after dinner we set off for Corvallis. The traffic was heavy and constant in both directions on the four-lane highway. Along the way we learned that Thanksgiving is the most important holiday in the U.S., even more so than Christmas. Americans don't recognize Boxing Day as a holiday like the rest of the civilized world and Thanksgiving is their annual four day long weekend. Neil and I did most of the talking as we motored along. Gary being gracious as always sat back as my old friend and I caught up during the drive. Gary was not kept out of conversations over the next few days but he knew that Neil and I had ground to cover and he let us cover it without ever getting his nose out of joint. He is a very good friend.

Corvallis

We arrived in Corvallis around nine that night. I had last seen Neil's wife, Azizah, son Johan and daughter Amelia nearly 10 years past when they had stayed overnight with me in Winnipeg. We received a warm welcome from Azizah and Johan. Amelia, an articling law student who lived in Portland, would arrive the next day. As Neil felt the need to prepare some of the menu for the morrow we all sat around the kitchen island. While enjoying wine and conversation Gary peeled apples for pies and I peeled potatoes. Our host took our output and created two apple pies and a potato dish then boiled up some fresh cranberries into sauce. He also prized the lids off a couple of tins for pumpkin pie.

The sampling of Neil's cellar dedicated to the wines of Oregon began in earnest that evening. He had a friend in the east with whom he corresponded regularly to discuss their shared interest in the grape. The passing of ideas and suggestions back and forth resulted in Neil accumulating a stock kept very handily in wine coolers in the three season room just off the living room. He had become quite enamored and knowledgeable about wine since our Manor St. David days of the early 1970's (Said wine was an unassuming but possibly immature Canadian sauterne that could be had for $1.90 a gallon, and regularly was).

Wine tasting with Neil was quite different than the one experienced on The Coast Starlight. On the train a dozen folks sampled four bottles while at Neil's three sampled a dozen.

It had been a great last day on the train and a fabulous evening but I was happy to find my bed just after 1:00am. Before nodding off I spent time updating my journal and thinking back on my long friendship with Neil. He was always a good man and I value his friendship. He has had his fair share of success in life but still remains much as he was when he, Dave, Ross, Danny, Helmut and I were 20 year olds having a good time doing all the stupid and careless things you do when you are invincible. My greatest memories are of group camping weekends at Falcon Lake when more than half a dozen of us would head out with tents, coolers, Extra Old Stock beer, cheap wine and remarkably little in the way of food. Neil had an old army tent that was big enough to park a car. Stuffing that monstrosity into the trunk of his Mustang after the weekend was always an engineering feat, especially if the tent was wet.

In those days Neil was easygoing with no pretentions and that is the way he remains. He always enjoyed the finer things in life but was also quite happy with the simplest and that I have always admired. We learned that evening that he'd had a personal setback the previous week and it was clouding his life. I hoped that the evening and the couple of days to come would help to lift those clouds a mite.

I slept the sleep of the dead no doubt helped along by a belly full of fine Oregon wine.

November 24, Thursday, American Thanksgiving

Neil and Azizah's home was situated on eight acres with the house on the highest point of a small hill. A long curved driveway meant the house couldn't be seen from the road. A good portion of their property was fenced as Azizah kept pets, all of which had names. She had eight alpacas and three goats and the menagerie were visited daily by a couple of deer. The fencing clearly kept the tame animals in but didn't seem to keep wild animals out. There was also a ginger cat wandering about the house. Neil also kept a herd of 50 Black Angus cattle at a nearby 80-acre ranch that was somehow intertwined with his business. It was quite the bucolic lifestyle.

The house was a larger two storey with the master on the main floor and all other bedrooms on the upper level at the other end of the home. The room I was staying in overlooked the backyard and a neighbouring property. A quarter of a mile in the distance another neighbour had a two-storey newer building that I took for a barn. Neil later told us it was an aquarium that the owner had built for his personal enjoyment. Can you imagine trying to clean the glass of that aquarium? The one we visited in Albuquerque had a couple of full time staff who with the aid of scuba equipment spent their entire day scrubbing glass walls while being watched over by lip-smacking sharks.

Thankfully Gary and I were in close proximity to a washing machine and by 9:30am we had arm wrestled to see who got to do laundry first. It is funny how important a washing machine can be. My dad always said you never realize the value of a glass of water until there isn't one around. The same can be said for clean socks and other things on an extended trip. After the laundry chores were completed we were good to go for the rest of the holiday.

Amelia arrived from Portland mid morning and Azizah was so happy to see her that they spent most of the day on the floor in front of the fireplace talking. While those two were catching up we watched Neil continue preparations for the holiday meal. He had us helping out a bit making a Swedish potato pancake, the recipe of which he carried from family rural roots in Saskatchewan. Basically you cook six potatoes and let them cool, then add a cup of butter and flour to the mix until it is the desired consistency which I am unable to adequately describe in writing. Then you roll them out and cook them on a flat top. They were delicious and the family all waited in anticipation as he cooked them. We made a couple of dozen and they were eaten with butter or plain while warm and they would take the place of bread at dinner.

Once the preliminary cooking was completed the day's work began. Neil had told us the hired hand who looked after the cattle had graciously been granted the holiday and was off to see family a couple of hours away. That left it to Neil to ensure the cattle were fed daily while he was gone. Gary and I were up for the adventure and we headed off to the ranch eight miles away just before 1:00pm. There seemed to be a lot off eights in Neil's life; eight acre home, 80 acre ranch, eight miles away.

It was a beautiful day although it clearly had been raining quite a bit recently as everything was soaking wet. The trip to the ranch only took a few minutes which was long enough to learn that Neil's company does research with the cattle on the ranch. There was also a relationship with the university and students were sometimes there undertaking their own research. In addition to the hired hand the company had a research scientist on the payroll.

As you entered the property left of the highway, a farm gate crossing the road prevented cattle escaping from fields or pastures. The entire property was fenced, which at 80 acres must have been a big job. We travelled down the approach road for only ten or so metres before we entered the main yard. If you can imagine a square, by going to the left directly at the foot of the access road were three old wooden outbuildings for storage of equipment and such. Continuing right around the square directly opposite the driveway entrance was a newer open-walled barn for the cattle. Following along right was a dirt road leading to the back of the property and next to the roadway were a couple of smaller new wooded sheds that staff used to change to work clothes and rubber boots. Next to this and completing the square was the old home site.

This had once been a family ranch and the home on the property had occupied land that appeared to be the size of a suburban plot. You could yet see the remains of landscaping. The house had long since been removed but there were still ornamental bushes and hedges and remains of sidewalks about. It appeared as if the house had just magically disappeared. There was a certain type of evidence that cattle had access to this piece of the land although there was fencing meant to keep them out. It seemed a very efficient set up to my untrained eye.

The stock included 12 calves, 37 mature cows and a solitary bull, who must have been quite happy. There were only calves in the barn when we arrived and the rest of the herd could be seen in the various fenced fields back of the barn. The pastures were on a rolling landscape with a fair number of treed areas and it was quite nice compared to our treeless landscape back home. You'll notice I shuffle between the terms fields and pastures. This is to hedge my bets around using the correct term for grass-covered patches of open land.

We were there to feed the cattle and before we proceeded Neil suggested Gary and I put on some rubber boots. It had been raining for a week and the ground was sodden and puddles were everywhere plus 50-odd cattle or so had the run of the place, if you get my drift. Gary at first said he didn't need to change footwear. He does take great care in how he looks while generally I stand accused of not having such inhibitions. In my working career I made many a farm visit and had learned the hard way if the farmer suggests rubber boots you are foolish to ignore the suggestion. While Neil could have cared less one way or the other I strongly impressed on Gary that he did indeed require rubber boots. I was quickly proved right.

By this time Neil had fired up the blue tractor which had hydraulic forks on the front end and had motored off into one of the buildings to pick up a huge bundle of hay. He was rumbling off down the mud track to the gate in the first pasture and shouted out to us to walk down and open the gate. It was like walking in a bog but we managed to get the gate open and let him onto the field and then we quickly closed the gate to prevent cattle escaping. The beasts scared the crap out of me and I didn't need them ambling by too close. Neil puttered off to the middle of the field toward a large round aluminum contraption where he deposited the bale of hay. The cattle would consume the bale in a day. He then came roaring back and we had to jump to get the gate open in time.

NEIL, THE COUNTRY GENTLEMAN, DOWN ON THE FARM

After putting the tractor away we looked around the barn at the assorted cattle and I knew right away that these were pets, not livestock. Neil claimed each animal was unique and recognizable. I for one could see little to differentiation one from another but Neil assured us that they each had their own personalities.

He and another old friend, Danny, had been quite the pranksters when we were kids. They were forever pulling gags on all of us and especially each other. There were instances when to get the upper hand one or the other would offer the other's furniture or car for sale in local newspapers, once from thousands of miles away. This past history made me question whether Neil was being serious or not now. It turns out he was and he could tell the different animals by sight. It was clear that Neil loved the ranch, the land and the animals and I took a picture of him on his tractor in all his glory.

Neil was a strange confluence of styles. He was well off enough that he could buy most anything he desired yet he loved his old beat up Toyota Land Cruiser. It had just experienced a life-altering happenstance and now he was driving a decades old Ford pickup. He also clearly enjoyed moving hay bales around the ranch with his tractor and his fashion sense could rightly be called very casual. He even wore those half moon reading glasses you can pick up at the drug store for a couple of bucks because he was forever losing his prescription ones. Yet he had a Rolex watch he wore all the time including when mucking out stalls in the barn. It was an odd juxtaposition; pitchfork in hand and Rolex on wrist.

When we were done with cows we took a sightseeing drive through Neil's hometown for much of the last three decades. We drove past his first home in Corvallis which was also on a hill up a winding road with a great covering of tall trees. This area was a more residential area than his present one with the houses situated on normal-sized city type lots and it was quite nice. It appeared to be a beautiful home but Neil said a friend of Azizah had called one day out of the blue about a place that she must see right away. They weren't really looking for a home but she saw it, loved it and they bought it. That had always been Neil's way - quick decisions, dive right in, damn the torpedoes and full speed ahead.

He also drove us through Corvallis proper and then through the university campus where he'd been a professor. While Neil had retired from the university a few years back it was obvious from the way he talked and the way we wandered about the campus that he'd enjoyed his time there. Gary and I were amazed at the campus football stadium, which could accommodate 50,000 fans. We are presently building a new 33,000-seat football stadium for our professional Canadian Football League team, the Winnipeg Blue Bombers, and there'd been all sorts of trouble raising the financing. The Corvallis stadium was for a university league and yet was nearly twice as big.

There was another interesting tidbit about football and home. The university coach had at one time coached our Big Blue. He was the son of a previous coach and had led our team to the league championship as a young man and then moved on for more money in the American college system. He had always been well loved in Winnipeg but apparently the bloom was off the rose in Corvallis. If the team did not do well at the big game on the upcoming weekend his job was tenuous at best.

It struck me as we were driving around how our lives had been so completely separate from each other for so many years and yet they were so similar. Relationships, kids, the hammering out of a career and making lives for ourselves and our families. I continue to be grateful that we had stayed in touch over the years and remained friends. Many don't make the effort and it is a shame that you can let go of your past so easily.

We were soon back at home with dinner preparations underway in earnest. Neil was doing most of it and supervising everything else. Azizah and Amelia remained on the floor in the living room in front of the fire while Johan, who'd had a late night, was still asleep. Gary and I were sitting around the kitchen island regularly jumping to Neil's instructions and enjoying seemingly endless bottles of wine. The evening would have another guest. Angie was an old friend from the previous neighbourhood who had moved to Oregon 20 years ago from England but still retained much of her accent. After a fabulous turkey dinner at which I got to know Neil's two wonderful children better we "retired to the drawing room" as my dad would say nightly. We spent the evening drinking wine, talking old and new times and listening to Neil's eclectic musical tastes emanating somehow from his lap top computer.

Then trouble.

Well into the after dinner festivities Neil received a phone call from a neighbour at the ranch. She told him that most of his herd had ambled off his property. The neighbour advised the herd had found a break in the fencing near a creek and were now on her property and would he kindly make arrangements to shift them.

Neil was gob smacked as you can imagine: his hired hand was away, the house was full of guests, we had just completed a big dinner and we were working relentlessly to sample as many Oregon wines as was humanly possible. The thought of wandering about in the dark to find and then chase 50 cattle through a break in a wire fence seemed an unlikely prospect for completion just then so he decided to wait until the light of day.

This was not the first time there had been a mass escape onto this particular neighbour's property and in the past she had been short tempered and unpleasant. I am sure that the thought of the cattle on her property was on his mind for the remainder of the evening but there was nothing for it but to wait for the sun to come up. We continued to enjoy the evening knowing that we would be chasing cows on the morrow.

This wasn't the first time Gary and I had an incident with wayward cows. While meandering through a cattle populated pasture on our England trip we had been eyed quite aggressively by a black bull who had made some threatening gestures that culminated in our leaping a barbed wire fence like school boys to effect an escape. It was only after we made good our escape that I noticed that Gary was wearing a red plastic bag over his hat to fend off rain.

We learned later that the issue of cattle being on a neighbouring field, while annoying, was not primarily because of any damage the trespassers might do. Rather it involved the reproductive cycles of the beasts. I hope I have that right as animal husbandry was never something I paid much attention to. Each rancher plans within reason when to have cows inseminated as apparently it's easiest to have the whole herd pregnant at the same time to economize on costs and veterinarian bills. I took that to mean that each individual rancher determines when the timing is best for his herd, rather than just let nature take its course. The neighbour's concern was that some of her herd might get knocked up. This would not only upset timetables but also there was a possible issue with unwanted and or inferior bloodlines being mixed and one of Neil's escaped animals was a bull. Apparently a bull in with heifers of another herd even for a short period was not a good thing.

But there was nothing that could be done that evening and as uncomfortable as the call was Neil put it right behind him. We spent the rest of the evening reminiscing about past times and lives lived. One story that came out of nowhere was from when we were 16. Our friend Danny had bought a Honda 50 step-through motorbike that set us off down the motorcycle road - a road I have yet to come to the end of. I soon had a Honda S90 purchased from Danny and Neil had a Yamaha Twinjet 100. Smaller engine capacities would have been hard to find but we loved the freedom that came our way. I recall trying to learn how to do wheelies in Neil's back lane one hot lazy afternoon. On another weekend we loaded the bikes up into a trailer and a bunch of us went out to another friend's family cottage at Lake of the Woods, about 160 km east of home. At the end of the weekend we learned the trailer with the bikes would not be returning for a few days. This did not sit well with Neil, who decided he would ride the little Yamaha back home down the Trans Canada Highway. The machine would barely do 90 km/h flat out and the trip took him the better part of the day, including a flat tire along the way. Neil never had another bike after that one and after a ride like that I could well justify an abhorrence of motorcycles. That said he always had a love of cars and in addition to muscle cars and a fling with an MG he once owned a Cadillac two-door coupe. I believe this model was the longest car ever made, so long it would not fit in his garage. He owned it for years and said the kids loved getting picked up from school in it. I would guess the back bumper of the car would still be on his property when he drove up to the school.

We had a great evening and though Gary was not party to the adventures that were brought up I was confident he did not feel left out. Before falling asleep that night I noticed a folding combination knife on the side table beside my bed. I had the same type of knife in the glove compartment of my old pickup truck back home. It is amazing the bits and pieces of home you can see anywhere if you just take the time to look.

November 25, Friday

8am on a beautiful sunny morning in Oregon and it was cow chasing time. Due to the reported mass break out of the Black Angus gang any tentative plans for the day were obviously postponed. After a quick bite and a cup of coffee we were on our way. Neil was clearly concerned about the loose cattle situation but was more concerned about the neighbour. There was a bit of history between them when it came to cattle getting out and he considered them not to be on the best of terms.

We were met at the ranch by the company's research scientist who, when Neil had called the night before, had offered to help with the round up. I'm sure the offer was heartfelt but in retrospect what could he do, the hired hand was 300 km away and the boss was calling. After quick introductions and the putting on of rubber boots (with no hesitation from Gary this time) we were off.

Then the damndest thing happened. Lo and behold, all the cattle were back in the barn except for half a dozen that were in an adjoining pasture. All present and accounted for. They were hungry and I guessed that the clever beasts knew where their next meal was coming from. To suggest Neil was flummoxed would be an understatement.

After making sure they were fed and that all gates were closed, as we came upon them we wandered into the centre of the property. Neil had decided the best course of action was to split up and wander beside the fence and ultimately meet again on the other side of the property. This approach was similar to the tale of how they set the borders on the jointly held French and Dutch Caribbean island of St. Maarten. The story goes that when deciding how to split the island between the two colonizing European countries a Dutchman and a Frenchman set out in opposite directions from a point on the coast. When they met up on the other side of the island a line would be drawn overland between the starting and ending spots and that would thereafter be the border. The legend goes that one of them sat down for a drink or two resulting in the division of the island ending up being less than equal. The Dutch got the south bit and the French got the northern part which is a larger piece of real estate. The French are known for wine and the Dutch for beer, there is a lesson there I think.

Gary and I headed to the right with Neil and our new friend going off to the left. The fence had been erected around the entire property just a few years prior so the walk beside the fencing was unencumbered by vegetation for the most part. The land was a fairly rolling landscape with occasional creeks and gullies that called for careful foot placement and there were three or four fenced pastures on the property that we had to pass through on our search. Apparently good animal husbandry calls for wise use of pastures to ensure the grasses don't get over munched and I imagine sometimes there is also a need to separate portions of the stock. We were old hands at navigating livestock-populated fields and knew well to keep track of the stuff scattered by 50 cattle when stepping forward. We managed to circumnavigate our half of the property without finding any broken fence nor slipping on to our backsides.

It was a beautiful warm morning with the sun shining and birds chirping, and to pass the time we had a ridiculous discussion about why I wear my watch on my right wrist. Gary insisted the proper place to wear a watch was on the left. He acknowledged that many left-handed people wear their timepiece on the right but insisted that I, being right handed, should wear it on my left. He is a stickler for convention is my old friend. I pointed out that wearing a watch on the right wrist allows for the checking of the time very conveniently. It is an almost fluid motion if one needs to ascertain the time whilst writing, for instance. Also, if it was acceptable for left-handed people to wear a watch on the right why the discrimination against a right-handed person doing the same? He gave up in exasperation, continuing to think me wrong but apparently prepared to live with the error of my ways.

Our two groups eventually met with neither of us finding any evidence as to how or where the cows escaped. Just as confusing was if they had in fact escaped how was it that they were all back where they were supposed to be? It was a puzzler. Perhaps the neighbour was playing a trick, could it have been somebody else's herd, had she had a nip at a bottle of rum? There was nothing for it but to call on the neighbour despite Neil's obvious trepidation. She lived right next door so we piled in the truck and drove over. Cowards that we were we waited in the truck while Neil bucked up and went to face the music. He was gone about 10 minutes and when back he related that she really was a nice person after all. It turned out that the herd had not escaped through his fencing but had escaped through the neighbour's fence. I know, it didn't make any sense to us either but I will try to make it as clear as my limited skills allow.

Armed with directions to the offending fence we immediately headed back to the barn. Neil got out his four-wheel, and this is important, one-person ATV and with me sitting on the rear metal rack holding on for dear life we bounced off across the muddy pastures headed to where Neil now knew the problem lay. I mention that we hit every pothole, puddle and mud pit along the way and I suspect my old chum was having a bit of fun. Once we got to the spot where the two properties met we immediately saw the problem. A fallen tree lay across a piece of the neighbour's fence and the wire was pressed down almost to the ground. We headed back to the barn for a chainsaw and the subsequent return was even more precarious. I now had to hold on with one hand and hold the chainsaw with the other all the while trying not to fall off, drop the saw, or cut either one of us with the chain blade, all the while trying to stay reasonably clean(ish). Neil again ensured we hit every possible hole and wet spot.

The problem area was where they had built the fence alongside some trees and brush at a point where the neighbour's property butted against this section of fence. Neil's portion of fence was not built along the property line as such but as more of a barricade to keep the cattle out of some brush. When the fence had been put up the thinking was that there no way a cow could wander in between the brush and the fence. Well, the thinking was wrong. The lead cow, clearly a very clever thing, had spied the downed fence. Then she and all her friends had single filed their way between the brush and Neil's fence and stepped over the neighbour's downed fence, which was conveniently pressed down to a height comfortable for a cow to step over. This was remarkable in itself as the pathway they took was barely a metre wide between fence and brush. For those of you who are unawares a cow is likely a metre wide. The truly remarkable thing was that some cow had seen the downed fence, got the idea for a free meal and went for it leading her friends along to munch their way through dinner on the neighbour's dime. Then they returned the way they had come to be home in time for breakfast. Cows no longer seemed as dim as I had once perceived.

Neil was amazed when he'd determined what had transpired and shaking his head jumped the fence and had the tree cut up and fence back in place in less than five minutes. The return journey to the barn was as hazardous as the others and I was covered in mud when we finally parked the ATV. Gary had all the while been wandering about the farmyard in the sunshine and was not in any way upset that he had missed out.

Now that work for the day had been concluded we headed to where Neil kept his airplane. He'd had the plane for a number of years and kept the sporty little 60 year old number at a private airfield. The place had rows of metal clad buildings with enormous garage doors for each individual hanger. Neil had offered to take us up for a flight to Mount Hood but as a coward when it comes to small airplanes I deferred. I am unsure if Gary wanted to go but it was moot as there was no way I was going. In my defense Neil had regaled us with a number of stories of hair-raising incidents of cloud banks so thick you couldn't see the mountains you were flying through, icing up of wings and unexpected landings that would have unnerved any rational being.

THE PLANE

Neil also told us that he had flown his airplane around Mount St. Helen's, the one that erupted and exploded in 1980. I recalled driving down Ellice Avenue towards an appointment downtown when suddenly the front window of my car was covered in a fine dust. I had a devil of a time getting my window washer and wipers to clean off the dust from that volcanic eruption halfway across the continent.

After I put the skids to a flight we had a quick look around then headed into town for lunch at another of Neil's favourite places. Then the plan was to head back home for a quick clean up then off to an aviation museum on the way out towards Portland.

The best laid plans...................., yet again.

We were back home by 4:00pm and were pretty well worn out from cow chasing and the fence fixing so we put off the museum visit. We were sitting around shooting the breeze when an upset Azizah came into the living room. She had been out in the yard tending to her pets when she'd found Renaldo the alpaca passed away in its little barn. More animal husbandry was in store for us.

We all jumped up and went out to have a look see. Actually Neil was doing the look see and we two were providing moral support some steps back. Arguably we were standing back to keep out of the way, although a dead alpaca had some unspoken concerns for both of us. Unhappily Azizah was right and the poor thing was dead. Neil, ever in charge, grabbed the beast by the back legs and dragged it 20 metres through the bush to the pickup truck. Then the three of us hefted the 40 kg dead weight (pardon that) into the bed of the truck and headed out to the landfill. All the way Neil the scientist was musing about what could possibly have happened, a fight with some of the other animals, some undiagnosed problem or an infection of some sort. In short order we were at the landfill and it was quite clear Neil had been on similar journeys before. The lack of reaction by the person manning the gate when Neil said he was dropping of a dead alpaca suggested it was not an uncommon thing. We drove to the top of a small hill and Neil backed the truck into place between two other trucks whose owners were also dropping of the detritus of life. Nobody batted an eye at our load and happily Neil managed the unloading by himself.

That evening Gary and I decided to treat our hosts to a meal, though only Neil and Johan were available to take us up on it. Neil picked his favourite pizza joint in Corvallis, Great American Pizza, which he usually gets to once a week . It was a bit of a funky place. You enter and immediately order and pay at the counter then find yourself a table. I always worry in such circumstances that after laying out the cash I might be unable to find a place to sit but no such bother this night. When the meal was ready a server came out of the kitchen and shouted out the name of who belonged to the pizza and said person shouted back "here" in response and I do mean shouted. Ever a traditionalist I had pepperoni while Neil, Johan and Gary each had some sort of New Age pie that I paid no attention to. It was delicious and the beer wasn't bad either. U.S. President Obama ate here during his first presidential campaign and we learned later that evening that Michelle Obama's brother teaches basketball in town at one of the high schools and that she is a frequent visitor to Corvallis.

Over dinner it was decided we would stop at a car lot on the way home. When we were young and foolish Neil had a couple of Mustangs, a 1965 and 1972 that he ran the you know what out of. In the past few years, in an effort to recapture his youth as we all do, he had bought similar cars. The older one had been hot rodded so much that he found it annoying to drive and Johan drove the other one daily. Neil was presently inclined to buy his son a new car as the 40 year old clapped out one needed work and was not deemed as safe as he would have liked. Apparently road trips up to Portland were a common occurrence for the young guy and his friends. It wasn't that the car was unsafe as Neil would readily have driven it but all parents put up with things we won't in any way accept as good enough for our children.

The car Johan had his eye on was a blue Mustang GT with white racing stripes. It was right up old Neil's street. As soon as we saw it I knew Neil liked it and I wondered who would be driving it if they bought it. Johan's 17th birthday was coming up and this would make a great gift and it was decided that we would all come back the next day for a test drive. It turned out calmer heads would prevail. A test drive was taken and the car was a hit but Johan's sister later calmly discussed the pros and cons of buying a muscle car around concerns with interior space, gas mileage and overall safety; it was decided not to proceed with that particular car. Shortly thereafter Johan became enamoured with a Subaru that caught his eye. It was sporty and economical at the same time and I imagine his sister gave her blessings as a purchase was made.

When we returned home from pizza and car browsing we spent the balance of the evening again talking old times, new times and the problems of the world with the aid of another four bottles from Neil's endless cellar. Gary staggered off to bed at some point while my old friend and I spent the early hours of the night, actually early morning, reminiscing about our late teens and early 20s when we were reckless and free of responsibilities. Our friend Danny is struggling with the horror of multiple sclerosis and we spent a goodly amount of time remembering much happier days with him. He was first stricken with symptoms in his mid 20s and continuing deterioration of his body has followed, not though his mind.

As teenagers Danny had been the front and centre of our little group. He was always the catalyst for new relationships in our tight but occasionally expandable group of friends and always seemed to have the brightest ideas around new adventures. I'd recently been reminded of the summer of 1973 by another old friend who's popped back into my line of sight after two decades. Danny had convinced Ray to take parachute lessons that year and they would jump out of an airplane seven times over the course of the summer. On one of those occasions Danny decided that just for the experience he would rely on his reserve chute rather than his main chute. The reserve chute worked well enough that day. As an aside to the tale and to show how far our society has come in 40 years, Ray told me that on their first ever jump a young woman who was to go before them climbed out on to the step then promptly changed her mind. However, she froze in place and the instructor could not drag her back in the plane as she refused to let go of the wing strut she was hanging on to. This was serious as they couldn't very well land with her standing out there. After all else failed the instructor began to hammer on her hands with his fist until she ultimately let go and gravity did the rest. Danny and Ray then jumped out after her.

Dave and I visit Danny in hospital every few months although it is not often enough. We are always touched by the joy in his eyes when he sets them upon us. He has nearly lost all ability to speak but he always starts our visit by telling a joke and if another old friend that he hasn't seen in some time tags along he always asks how much money he makes. Invariably when we take him for a coffee he requests that I buy him a type of pastry to go with his Earl Grey tea knowing full well the pastry he requests is not available. He takes pleasure in having me ask the server for the nonexistent treat and always makes me pick up the tab.

It is bittersweet 40 years on to look back at your teens with joy and happiness at those people who were so much a part of your life and who helped shape you without even knowing or trying to. Danny taught us how to live life then and especially now.

Neil returned to Winnipeg in late winter 2012 for a few days and he visited Danny with Dave and I. It was a beautiful visit and meant a lot to all four of us.

When I finally fell into bed I was beat and worn out but extremely happy. I slept like a king, again helped along by Neil's cellar. It was an amazing thing that the wine we were drinking never produced trouble the next morning. A lifetime of experience suggests there is a relationship between the quality of the next morning and the quality of the wine drunk the night before, notwithstanding the quantity utilized. Neil's cellar was of a higher quality than either Gary or I was used to imbibing. It's not that I don't enjoy fine wine it was just that I seldom put such good wine away in the quantities I was putting away in Corvallis. Bless our host's generosity.

November 26, Saturday, last day in Corvallis and heading for Portland

Up at 8:00am and what a visit it had been. We spent hours talking old times, friends and loved ones here and gone and the magic of how lives move away and then come back. We laughed about school, work, careers, cars, books, music, booze and our kids, and Neil quite willingly allowed us to put a huge dent in his wine stocks. We spent time doing everyday simple things and we helped with and enjoyed a huge and delicious Thanksgiving celebration, one that I was particularly thankful for. We had a terrific pizza in a joint we would never have found on our own and chased cows around a muddy soaking field plus dealt with the passing of a family pet. Gary had willingly and without rancor stepped back a bit to allow Neil and I to catch up on the past 35 years. I found Neil remarkably unchanged since we were kids and in spite of a full life lived these many years he was still the same 19 year old I used to share a drink and high times with. Success had allowed him to indulge in anything he wished and he shares his good fortune unflinchingly. His real success can be seen in his wonderful family, all happy and content.

The morning plan was for a quick coffee, off to the ranch to feed the cattle then breakfast at The Bad Egg. Before jumping in the truck Neil took us, coffee in hand, for a tour around his yard. I noticed he didn't think twice about leaving car keys in vehicles nor was he concerned about locking the house doors at night. It was kind of nice. It had only been a week since Albuquerque where drug stores, gas stations and fast food places all felt the need for security guards on duty when doors were open. When I was young my dad used to leave the car keys under the floor mat in the front seat no matter if the car was at home, work or the pub. They were always under the mat. I also don't recall seeing keys for our house until the 1970s and I don't remember ever having a house key in my pocket. We would go on vacation and the doors would be unlocked for weeks at a time. I don't know if it was any safer back then but we certainly were not as worried about things happening as we seem to be today.

Neil's property as I mentioned earlier was built on a small hill with the house at the crown hidden from the road by a grove of trees. The driveway to the house was in the centre of the property and on either side were lush green lawns manicured in some part by alpacas and goats. On the right side of the property were a couple of fast-running creeks coursing through the trees. There was even a swimming hole his kids used to splash about in. A couple of the creeks merged further back in an area that was more heavily bushed with foot paths and small wooden bridges over the running water. The bush area was not maintained and it seemed quite wild when you were in there and with the sound of the rushing water and chirps of birds it seemed like being out in the woods, not just 30 metres from the house. As we wandered around to the back the path opened up onto another lush lawn but first we had to wend our way around a pond that was fed by an incoming stream. It was a beautiful spot and Neil was clearly at peace when walking about.

THE AUTHOR IN OUR HOST'S BACK GARDEN

The tour completed, we jumped in the truck for the quick trip to the ranch for the feeding of cows that went off without a hitch and then off we went to breakfast. That was a good thing as we were all getting a little peckish. Corvallis is a university town so there were a lot of funky places to dine and The Bad Egg was no exception.

Neil said that he hit the hippy dippy joint a couple of times a week. When I got home it struck me that Neil seemed to have a lot of eateries that he told us he frequented weekly. Michelle Obama had also dined at this place that was clearly set up on the cheap in an old retail store in a long block of buildings in the centre of town. We were all ravenous and would have eaten deep fried cardboard by this time but happily the breakfast was great and plentiful. I had corned beef hash which is a favourite but not always so nicely prepared. Over breakfast we made plans to head off to Portland in the late afternoon and along the way stop in at the aviation museum we had put off visiting the previous day. When we got back from breakfast Amelia had already headed back to Portland and Johan still being 17 was still in bed.

We were home in time to begin watching the Civil War football game on television. Oregon has two universities, Oregon State University at Corvallis and the University of Oregon in Eugene. The famous game was first played in 1894 and except for five years it had been played annually ever since. It had been commonly known as the Civil War since 1929 with games played on even years in Corvallis and Eugene in odd years. It was a state rivalry, hence the name, and this game was especially more important than most. This was the season-decider, with the winner going on to the Rose Bowl and the loser going home. Fortunately for us we would be heading out for Portland prior to the end of the game. Neil and Azizah were cheering for different teams so somebody was going to be unhappy.

Shortly after 3:00pm and with great thanks we said our goodbyes to Azizah and began the two hour drive in glorious sunshine with a plan to motor down a less-travelled highway to take in the Evergreen Aviation & Space Museum in McMinnville, Oregon. This museum was the work of Captain Michael King Smith, the son of Delford M. Smith who at one time had the largest fleet of 747s in the world. The elder Smith started with one helicopter after World War II and expanded to ultimately end up ferrying U.S. armed forces personnel to hotspots around the world.

The road less travelled apparently was a good idea for a good many folks at the end of the Thanksgiving weekend. At times it was bumper to bumper. The first part of the journey in daylight was very nice as we travelled through rolling hill country with vineyards and wineries everywhere you looked. It was not quite the same thing but it did remind me of a trip to southeast France a number of years ago when Gary, Kim, Lynn and I stayed at a cousin's farm cottage vacation home near Toulouse. This time we didn't stop to take advantage of buying some delicious plonk right out of the barrel at a roadside winery dispensed by a willowy long-legged dark-haired young French beauty.

Along the way we saw famous Mount Hood, one of the loftiest peaks in the country. It was snowcapped and Neil said it was always so. The mountain was a popular spot for outdoor adventures and unfortunately there are a number of fatalities each year as people reached beyond their grasp. It is a good thing to try to exceed your grasp but it can be very sad if one fails. I had a thought then that it would have been a marvelous thing to have flown around Mount Hood in Neil's plane and maybe I should have been stronger when the opportunity presented itself.

Then again, maybe not. As I was finalizing this little tale I received a harrowing account from Neil about a flight Johan and he had tried to make to Seattle for a Neil Young concert. In another of life's coincidences my Sara was taking me to a concert on the same tour a week after the one they were set to attend.

The battery on the airplane had been flat when they arrived so as with a car they arranged a boost and were soon up and running. After all the routine checks were completed they were on their way up into the wild blue yonder or wild black yonder since it was dark when they finally took off. Shortly after they were up electrical components started to fail and soon they had no lights nor instruments but more importantly they'd lost the electrical power needed to lower the landing gear. It must have been frightening for Neil with his son sitting beside him. In great detail Neil described how he managed the emergency to ultimately arrive back on

Mother Earth safe and sound. I have never had trouble speeding all over on my motorbike and used to consider smugly that I was fearless, well I am not.

It was just getting to dusk when we reached the aviation museum. The complex consisted of three enormous buildings built along the lines of aircraft hangers with glass fronts and rears. The first building housed a water slide park as I guess not everyone is content just looking at airplanes. The enormous building had a 747 parked on the roof three stories up. Kids of all ages take an elevator to the airplane perched on the roof like a giant canary then go out a door on the airplane to commence the downward ride on the waterslide. It was so incredible as to defy description and it stopped us in our tracks when we looked up at it.

The other buildings housed airplanes from throughout the years plus spacecraft and high altitude airplanes. The museum's pride of show was Howard Hughes' legendary Spruce Goose, which only flew one time to prove that Hughes was not a failure. The fact it only got a few metres off the surface of the water and never flew again is a fairly good argument to suggest it was in fact a failure. Nevertheless it was a remarkable airplane.

The second building contained airplanes from the very beginning of aviation history and we saw many that we recognized including one like Neil's suspended from the ceiling. Earlier Neil had been musing about getting rid of his as he didn't feel he used it enough but once he saw the one hanging from the ceiling he immediately changed his mind. There were airplanes from both sides of all of the armed conflicts of the 20th Century and also peacetime craft and racing machines. All were in perfect condition and you could walk right up to most of them. We snapped pictures like mad.

The third building housed the space exhibits, Titan missiles, space capsules and spy planes. We saw a spy plane built in 1961 that the world was unaware existed until the mid-70s - it looked right out of James Bond. We had earlier seen a commuter airplane also designed and built in 1961 that was considered to be the height of engineering at the time. Compared to the spy airplane it looked like it had been put together with stone hammers and bronze chisels. Imagine what is flying up there right now that we don't know about.

I have an English cousin named Gillian whose late husband Kim had loved airplanes and as I was wandering about I knew that he would have been tickled to have had the opportunity to have seen this place.

NEIL, ME AND THE SPRUCE GOOSE

By time we were on our way again it was 5:30pm and black as pitch out on the road. It was 100 km to Portland and soon we were in bumper to bumper traffic again. We were motoring along when a friend of Neil's from his Oregon life called. It seemed he'd had a very difficult time lately and just wanted to talk and Neil being ever gracious and helpful let him talk away for almost half an hour. Afterwards the three of us aimlessly chatted and covered all sorts of ground. This is where we learned that Neil's condo wasn't in

Portland nor even in Oregon. The condo was across the Columbia River from Portland in Vancouver, Washington.

We arrived at the condo complex of a dozen or so newly built buildings. Each unit had two floors, Neil's had three bedrooms and an attached garage. We quickly unloaded then headed out for a local brew pub overlooking the mighty Columbia from where we could see the lights of downtown Portland. As usual we were all ravenous so ate our dinners and supped our beers without too much ado. Since it had been awhile since Neil had used the condo and it is primarily used as a stopover around flights or as an overnight for shopping trips to Portland, we needed some supplies. We headed over to a large grocery store and picked up some coffee, cream, fruit, and buns for breakfast. Gary was looking ahead to making sure there was a next meal handy. Oh, and we also bought three very large bottles of a local craft beer called Arrogant Bastard IPA. We then headed back to the condo for the balance of the evening.

We soon tucked into the beer which was quite a strong brew and after the couple we had already put away with dinner Gary wandered off to bed around 10:00pm. Neil and I continued to sit around talking about the old days and where our lives were at. All the talking soon turned our throats dry and Neil discovered a half bottle of red wine that he assumed Amelia had opened on her last use of the place. We made short work of that. During our talk I learned that Johan was going over to Oxford for a five week university course in July and that started a conversation about a trip to Oxford and region that Lynn and I had made a few years ago. We continued on about old times and new, good times and bad, happy times and sad and somewhere along the way we discovered a bottle of spiced rum that was also put to good use, albeit with only water for mix. It went down remarkably smoothly. I am unsure what time we staggered off but I am reasonably sure that it was past 3:00am. As reasonably sure as one in my condition could have been about anything.

Home

November 27, Sunday, Portland and heading home

Six in the morning came awfully quick. We needed to be on our way within the hour and we weren't moving very fast. There is an old saying in my home town about how you feel after spending a night boozing. Put delicately, it involves a monkey watering your mouth whilst you sleep. That's how I felt and by the look of it Neil felt the same while Gary of course was as bright as a new penny. Over quick cups of coffee Neil mentioned that he was pretty sure we had discussed and solved all of the world's problems the previous evening but he was damned if he could recall any of our solutions.

We made our deadline of course and were soon on the way passing over bridges spanning the Columbia with a glorious view of Mount Hood's snow-packed peak all the while. Neil was an old hand at travelling to and from this airport and he swung into the extended parking lot right next to the shuttle pickup point. We had our bags out of the truck and had walked over to the pickup shed as the shuttle pulled up.

Neil was leaving first so we walked with him down to his gate and check in. He was off to that hot paradise of Hawaii and we were off to the cold paradise of Central Canada and no, it wasn't quite the same thing. Neil can fly to Hawaii in three and a half hours for a couple of hundred dollars with an upgrade to first class costing only a hundred more. My flight to Winnipeg from Portland would take most of a day and cost a damn sight more. Neil got checked in alright but there was a growing group of people milling about who were on their way to Honolulu. They were being told that their plane was delayed and chances were looking good that they would not be leaving that day at all. As a result, there was some consternation within the group.

We said our goodbyes. The stay with Neil and Azizah had been a great cap to a spectacular holiday.

By 8:00am we were at our gate awaiting the 10:20 flight to Vancouver. There was no option of arriving 30 minutes prior to departure on this piece of the journey. As usual Gary was chomping at the bit to get checked in as soon as possible and as was also usual he had an issue or two at the desk. I ended up somehow getting through first and then the same thing happened at security. Eventually we were comfortably ensconced for the quick hop to Vancouver, British Columbia not Washington. Then there were rumblings that the plane was going to be late. I didn't see that as an issue as my flight to Winnipeg was at 2:25pm but Gary's connection was an hour before mine. It looked like delays were going to cut into our final lunch.

The waiting lounge was a smallish room on the runway level of the airport and it was starting to fill up. With a flashback to Depew there seemed to be more of us than seats. Not only was the plane late but they had already called for volunteers to give up their seats for $200 and a later flight and we saw a couple of folks take advantage of the offer. All we could do was sit and read the papers until the plane arrived.

By 1:00pm we were in the Vancouver Airport which is one of the worst airports I have ever had the misfortune to pass through and true to form everything was a mess. Ah, to be on the train again. My bag was inexplicably first off the line but then the baggage carrousel suddenly stopped carouselling. The bulk of my fellow passengers could not get their bags and since we were already late most of them would have had to run to Customs to make connections if the carousel had been working, and Gary was one of those unfortunates. We had a very tense 20 minutes and this was not the way anyone wanted to end a holiday.

Eventually things started to move and when his bag arrived Gary had to make a beeline for the Customs gate. I however had plenty of time so decided to have lunch. Instead of a burger and Coke I opted for a Chinese rice and chicken dish from a kiosk and it turned out to be quite delicious. Six uneventful hours later I was home safe and sound and it was great to be with family once again.

It had been a terrific three weeks. We had seen and done lots and I had truly enjoyed the train ride itself. I would do it again in a heartbeat. Next time I would take the train around the circumference of the United States. Starting from Toronto I'd head to New York then down the eastern seaboard to Florida then track west along the Gulf and finally up the west coast to British Columbia. That would be a trip.

There was a great deal of time during the three weeks when I was alone with my thoughts. My journal started out as recounting of a pleasant and thoroughly enjoyable train ride with a good friend and the meeting up with an old friend at the journey's terminus. It turned into the reflective journey of many joyful chapters of a life lived. Wonderful memories from the past made even happier by reminiscing with two friends. Travelling and talking brought back long forgotten days.

A ride on a train triggered a ride through memories.

Epilogue

I learned later that Gary's day turned into 16 grueling hours of travelling and waiting. After the fright in Vancouver he travelled to Toronto, flying over Thunder Bay in order to catch a flight from Toronto back to Thunder Bay. He had arranged all the tickets in Vancouver because he was concerned about the limited amount of time he had between each and thinking he would not have any time to spare. On the Toronto flight the flight attendant even arranged for him to sit at the front so he could make like the old O.J. Simpson commercial and dash through the airport to make the connection to Thunder Bay. My apologies to anyone I might offended by mentioning O.J. It turned out that the Thunder Bay flight was two hours late leaving Toronto so he had more than enough time for a drink and to curse Air Canada.

Neil visited Winnipeg a few months later and related the story of a once in a hundred year flood in Corvallis. It seems the runoff from the high ground was much greater than usual and it flooded the ranch, over a third of a metre of water in the yard. It took five days for it to subside but the angels were watching over Neil. A cagey neighbour (not the one next door) at the ranch saw what was coming and moved Neil's cattle to higher ground for him.

Oh, and I threw my shoes away the minute I got home, but I kept the laces as there was nothing wrong with them.

The End

Printed in Canada